# SCHOLASTIC

# READ & RESPOND

## Bringing the best books to life in the classroom

# Guided Reading

## Key Stage 2

### Comprehensive guided reading notes for:

- **Kensuke's Kingdom**
- **Charlie and the Chocolate Factory**
- **Varjak Paw**
- **Holes**
- **The Amazing Maurice and His Educated Rodents**
- **War Horse**

AGES
9–10

Scholastic Education, an imprint of Scholastic Ltd
Book End, Range Road, Witney, Oxfordshire, OX29 0YD
Registered office: Westfield Road, Southam, Warwickshire CV47 0RA
www.scholastic.co.uk
© 2017, Scholastic Ltd
1 2 3 4 5 6 7 8 9     7 8 9 0 1 2 3 4 5 6

British Library Cataloguing-in-Publication Data
A catalogue record for this book is available from the British Library.
ISBN 978-1407-16949-1
Printed and bound by Ashford Colour Press

Due to the nature of the web we cannot guarantee the content or links of any site mentioned. We strongly recommend
that teachers check websites before using them in the classroom.

Every effort has been made to trace copyright holders for the works reproduced in this book, and the publishers
apologise for any inadvertent omissions.

Extracts from National Curriculum for England, English Programme of Study © Crown Copyright. Reproduced under the
terms of the Open Government Licence (OGL). www.nationalarchives.gov.uk/doc/open-government-licence/version/3/

**Authors** Sally Burt, Pam Dowson,  Eileen Jones, Samantha Pope and Debbie Ridgard
**Editorial** Rachel Morgan, Jenny Wilcox, Kate Buckley, Caroline Low, Margaret Eaton
**Cover and Series Design** Neil Salt and Nicolle Thomas
**Layout** Neil Salt

# CONTENTS

# ▼ INTRODUCTION

*Read & Respond* provides teaching ideas related to a specific children's book. The series focuses on best-loved books and brings you ways to use them to engage your class and enthuse them about reading. This book provides detailed guided reading sessions for six children's books.

## GUIDED READING

Guided reading is usually conducted in small groups with children of a similar reading ability, under teacher guidance. The groups are often around six to eight children, although may be fewer depending on the children in your class. The sessions are likely to be short, around 20 minutes, and focused on reading and comprehension skills.

There should be one focus text and each child should have a copy of it. The text should be slightly more challenging than the children's independent reading level, where they can read and understand the vast majority of the text independently. The teacher facilitation of guided reading allows for the children to access more challenging materials in a supported environment – they should still be able to understand and access 90 per cent of the content though.

Guided reading is much more than just reading in turns. Time should be given for reading independently; the teacher may wish to listen to individual children, but this should be followed up by checking the children's understanding and comprehension of the text through discussion and questioning.

### How this book relates to the *Read & Respond* teacher's book

This book can be used as stand-alone sessions or in conjunction with the corresponding *Read & Respond* teacher's books. Each *Read & Respond* teacher's book is designed for whole-class teaching and contains a variety of activities that look at grammar, punctuation and spelling; plot, character and setting; speaking and listening; and writing.

While there are guided reading notes in the teacher's book, the ones provided in this book are much more detailed and therefore the two books can work together. If you are using a carousel system for guided reading, then the teacher's book may provide supporting activities to use when the children are not in the guided reading group. Within this book, there may be some optional links referenced to the *Read & Respond* teacher's book, where work could be expanded.

## ABOUT THE BOOK

Each children's book has been divided into eight guided reading sessions. The sessions work through each book progressively, so you read it over a number of weeks. It has been assumed that the sessions will be conducted in guided reading groups of around six to eight children; if you plan to use them differently, then they can be adapted accordingly. Each session follows a similar structure:

**Session aims**: The purpose of the session and what children will be focused on in their reading.

**Before the session**: If there is anything the children need to do prior to the session, such as reading some of the book, this will be identified here.

**Read**: This section will focus on the children reading the text either independently or as a group. It may be reading new chapters or sections of the book or re-reading parts of the book that they have read previously. They should consider questions about the text while reading and then discuss these as a group to check their understanding.

**Revisit and respond**: A range of different activities will have been provided under this heading to provide flexibility to select appropriate tasks for the group. As each session is only intended to be around 20 minutes long, it is advised that one or two of these activity ideas are used to meet the needs of your children.

**Assessment opportunities:** A bank of questions has been provided which could be used at any point in the session as relevant. They are sub-divided into headings to identify the purpose of the type of question.

At the end of the book, you will find two templates that you can use to support your guided reading sessions:

**Guided Reading Bookmark Template**: This template provides a bookmark that you can complete and give to the children as reference. It could include the questions you want them to consider when reading or you could use the assessment opportunities questions for the children to discuss.

**Guided Reading Record Template**: A template to record any notes from a guided reading session so you have a record that you can refer to.

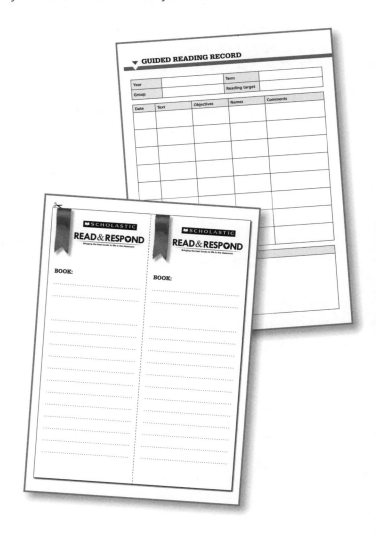

# ▼ SESSION 1: THE PEGGY SUE

## SESSION AIMS

Find out about the narrator of the story and learn the basis of the plot.
Consider questions relating to the title and the opening paragraphs.

## READ

- Ask the children to read the opening of the first chapter, up to 'as I knew him'.

- Encourage the children to think about all the questions the opening raises. Ask them: *How did the narrator disappear? Where did he go? How did he get back? Who is Kensuke? Why did Kensuke make the narrator promise to say 'nothing… until at least ten years had passed'?* Challenge the children to make predictions about what the answers might be.

- Draw the children's attention to the Chinese version of the chapter headings. Ask: *What clue does this give us?*

### During reading

- Ask the children to read to the end of Chapter 1. As they read, encourage them to compare Michael's family life before and after redundancy. Ask:
  - How did it affect Mum, Dad and Michael?
  - What was Dad's ultimate response that was to change their lives forever?

- Discuss the children's observations when they have finished reading.

- If your school uses reading journals then the children should be encouraged to make notes as they read and consider each question.

- Move around the group and 'tune in' to hear individuals read aloud. Encourage and praise good expression.

## REVISIT AND RESPOND

Use the following discussion points to help the children think about what they have read in more depth.

**Note:** Since there are only 20 minutes for each session, you are advised to focus on only one or two of the elements that are listed below.

- Ask the children: *What do you think about the idea of sailing around the world?* Discuss whether they think Michael's parents are behaving sensibly.

- Find predictions in the text of how things might turn out, both good and bad ('We could see places we've only ever dreamed of'; 'it's dangerous'; 'we'll be flat broke'; 'the adventure of a lifetime'; 'Icebergs, hurricanes, pirates, whales, supertankers, freak waves'). Encourage the children to make their own predictions about what might happen in the story.

- Ask the children to look again at the section where Michael describes his changing relationship with his parents once they are on board the *Peggy Sue*. Discuss Michael's discoveries about his parents and how he feels about them in their new circumstances.

- The author uses some challenging vocabulary, such as 'inculcated' and 'adamant'. Clarify these words with the children and ask them to keep an ongoing list of new vocabulary.

- Ask the children what nautical vocabulary they found during the independent reading – there is a lot of specific terminology ('dinghy', 'tiller', 'skipper', 'yachting marina', 'winches', 'helm', 'galley' and so on). Ask the children: *Why do you think the author uses this vocabulary?*

- Encourage the children to relate the text and the themes to their own lives/experiences. For example, you could ask them to imagine their parents/carers announce they are going to sail around the world, leaving their normal life behind. Discuss with the children how they and their extended family or friends would react. Would they take a mascot or lucky charm with them? What would it be? How would their pets react to living on board a boat?

Ask the children, whenever appropriate, to revisit the text to exemplify/support their answers.

Encourage the children to read aloud back to the group when referring back to the text – praise clear, confident and expressive reading.

### Before the next session
Ask the children to read Chapter 2. As they read, encourage them to think about how Michael's life has changed. Get them to to imagine themselves in Michael's situation and consider how they would cope.

## ASSESSMENT OPPORTUNITIES
The following bank of question prompts provides a quick and easy means of monitoring the children's comprehension skills and understanding of the text. The children's answers to a question must be supported by evidence from the text.

### Understanding
* What happened to Michael's father that made it possible for the family to go on their journey?
* Explain what happens to change Michael's life.
* How old is the narrator? (If he disappeared in 1988 at the age of 12, and more than 10 years have passed, he must be at least 22 years old.)
* Who were the four who lived in Michael's house?
* What was the name of Michael's school, and what did his dad call it?
* What job did Michael have?
* How did things change in the house after Michael's dad was made redundant?
* What had Michael's dad done that made mum so upset she cried?
* Where had Michael's dad gone?
* How does Michael's gran try to dissuade them from sailing off?
* What was the *Peggy Sue?*
* What was Michael's mum's reaction when dad told her about his plan?
* Who was going to be skipper of the boat?
* What was Michael's job on the boat?

* What would happen about Michael missing school while they were away on their adventure?
* How was Michael able to write in detail about everything that happened to them?
* What did Michael's friend Eddie Dodds give him as they left?

### Inferences
* Why has Michael 'had to live out a lie' for ten years?
* What do you think Michael is talking about when he refers to 'how I lived to come back from the dead'?
* Does Michael enjoy the family outings? How do you know?
* How does Michael's mother feel about moving home? Explain your answer.
* How does Michael feel about sailing around the world? How do you know?
* How do Michael's feelings about his parents change when they start to live on the *Peggy Sue*? Explain how you know.

### Predicting
* What do you think will happen when the journey begins? Will they be successful as sailors? Will the ship encounter any problems?

### Language, structure and presentation
* What is 'Blue water sailing'?
* Michael describes his mother as 'gritty'. What do you think he means by this?
* How do you feel when the narrator speaks of 'a creeping misery' in the house, how his parents argued 'a lot' when they had never done so before and how Michael 'tried to stay out of the house'.

### Themes and conventions
* Why do you think the story is written in the first person?

# ▼ SESSION 2: SHIP'S LOG

## SESSION AIMS

Identify how the author has deliberately changed his writing style to reflect the age of the narrator. Empathise with the main character.

## BEFORE THE SESSION

The children should have read Chapter 2 independently.

## READ

- Michael's mum teaches him navigation skills when they begin their journey. Ask the children: *Why might these skills be important for Michael?*

- Michael says he 'was always kept busy' and lists the tasks he had to do. The author likes lists and uses them often in this story. Suggest the children look out for this technique throughout the book and discuss the effect it has here (it conveys a sense of how busy everyone is on board).

- Michael says that Stella Artois was the 'greatest comfort', but note how important the football is to him. Ask the children to find references to the football and clarify these words with them: 'mascot', 'lucky charm', 'talisman'. Discuss why the football is important to Michael (it reminds him of his friends; he comes to associate it with surviving bad times).

- Discuss Michael's relationship with his mother once they started their journey.

- Ask the children: *What does Michael enjoy about sailing and what does he not enjoy? How would you feel if you were in Michael's situation? What would help you to cope? What would you miss the most?*

### During reading

- Continue the session by asking the children to read Chapter 3. As they read, encourage them to keep in mind the voice of the narrator as he writes his ship's log.

- Remind the children that the ship's log was written at the time of the voyage, when Michael was 11 years old, while Michael wrote the rest of the story at least ten years later.

- When they have finished reading, ask the children: *Does it sound as though an 11-year-old boy is writing the log? Explain your reasons.*

- If your school uses reading journals then the children should be encouraged to make notes as they read and consider each question.

- Move around the group and 'tune in' to hear individuals read aloud. Encourage and praise good expression.

## REVISIT AND RESPOND

Use the following discussion points to help the children think about what they have read in more depth.

**Note:** Since there are only 20 minutes for each session, you are advised to focus on only one or two of the elements that are listed below.

- Invite the children to skim and scan the chapter, to see if they can work out how many days the family have spent at sea since the start of their voyage.

- Michael's ship's log consists of nine selected entries that take us from September to July the next year (a period of nine months). Ask the children to look for the dates when Michael made the entries, then make a note of the date and where he was.

- Encourage the children to think about the style of writing in comparison with previous chapters. Ask: *Does it sound as though an 11-year-old boy is writing here?* Are the children able to see that the author has deliberately changed the way he writes? Encourage them to explain the difference in writing style between Chapter 3 and the first two chapters. (Chapter 3 has simpler language, shorter sentences and is very factual.)

- Ask the children to think about the journey. Which bits would they like to know more about? Make a list of questions to ask Michael, for example about the amazing places he visited or what sort of toilet they have on board.

- Encourage the children to think about what it would really be like to live on a boat for weeks and weeks. Remind them they would have no television, very little privacy and days and days of time to fill.

- Ask: *How many days do you think the family spent at sea?* Skim and scan to see if you can come up with a reasonable estimate. Then ask: *How long was the journey? How many days did they spend on land?*
- Consider why Michael's log ends so suddenly. What happened? Read aloud the last few pages (after the log has ended).

Ask the children, whenever appropriate, to revisit the text to exemplify/support their answers.

Encourage the children to read aloud back to the group when referring back to the text – praise clear, confident and expressive reading.

### Before the next session
Ask the children to use the map of the voyage at the end of the book as the basis for some research about the places Michael and his family visited.

Ask the children to read Chapter 4, up to 'We had survived'.

## ASSESSMENT OPPORTUNITIES

The following bank of question prompts provides a quick and easy means of monitoring the children's comprehension skills and understanding of the text. The children's answers to a question must be supported by evidence from the text.

### Understanding
- Where is Michael 'on watch' on 20 September?
- How long do they spend in La Coruña?
- Who only knew the English words 'Goal' and 'Manchester United'?
- Where have the family reached by 1 January?
- List the countries visited by the family.
- Name the animals, fish and birds that Michael records in the log from September to July.

### Inferences
- Why do you think Mum and Dad wouldn't let Michael do 'watch' for the first two nights of the voyage?
- Is the island of St Helena famous? How do you know?
- Is the 'man-overboard' drill helpful in the Indian Ocean? Explain your answer.

- Do all the family learn a lesson after Stella Artois goes overboard? Explain.
- 3 April is a significant day for the family. Explain how they are feeling and why the day is special.
- Why do you think Stella Artois is still barking into the darkness and 'reluctant' to move after the ball has disappeared?
- Why does Michael's log end so suddenly?

### Predicting
- What do you think happens next to Michael and his dog?

### Main ideas
- Do the entries in the ship's log persuade or discourage you from sailing or travelling by sea? Explain your answer.

### Language, structure and presentation
- Do you think the author's portrayal of an 11-year-old's ship's log is convincing? Explain your views.
- 'We saw gannets slicing into the sea.' Explain why you think the author uses the word 'slicing' here.
- Explain what is happening if you are 'becalmed' at sea.
- The narrator describes being suddenly 'in the cold of the sea before I could even open my mouth to scream' (page 44). Explain how you think the author wants you to feel here.

**SESSION 3:** GIBBONS AND GHOSTS

## SESSION AIMS

Consider how Michael reacts to events. Empathise with Michael in his new situation.

## BEFORE THE SESSION

The children should have read Chapter 4 up to 'We had survived'.

## READ

- Ask the children to consider the variety of emotions that Michael must have felt from when he realised the *Peggy Sue*, and his parents, were sailing away, up to the point where he had been reunited with Stella Artois and was thankful to have survived.

- Ask the children why the football had become so important to Michael. Was it just as a buoyancy aid, or something else as well?

- Michael's description of what he did and thought as he trod water sounds quite rational. For example, he realised it was pointless to waste energy by trying to swim and he sang to keep himself awake. Can the children explain this rationality at a time of intense distress?

- Ask the children: *Do you think Michael's decision to climb through the forest to a high point was a sensible thing to do? What alternatives did he have? What made Michael feel 'strangely elated'?*

### During reading

- Ask the children to read to the end of Chapter 4 independently.

- Invite the children to imagine how they would feel and what they would do in Michael's situation.

- If your school uses reading journals then the children should be encouraged to make notes as they read and consider each question.

- Move around the group and 'tune in' to hear individuals read aloud. Encourage and praise good expression.

## REVISIT AND RESPOND

Use the following discussion points to help the children think about what they have read in more depth.

**Note:** Since there are only 20 minutes for each session, you are advised to focus on only one or two of the elements that are listed below.

- What does Michael's discovery of food and water mean? What questions would he want to ask?

- When Michael gets to the peak of the hill he realises that he's on an island and begins to make plans. He knows he needs water and food. What else will he need?

- Re-read (or read aloud) from 'The howling had started up again'. Ask the children to list all the words and phrases to do with sound here and over the next two pages. Clarify the word 'mellifluous' – say it aloud and listen to the sound of the word. Point out how Michael Morpurgo uses lists of words that mean almost the same thing ('salty and brackish'; 'whirred and whined'; 'scraping, scratching, and a grunting'; 'exhilarated, elated, ecstatically happy'). What is the effect of this?

- While they were reading this chapter, had the children remembered that it is Michael's birthday?

- At the same time as Michael is wondering who or what has left him food, he is also delighted to have something to eat and drink. Would the children like to try raw fish and red bananas? Look at how the narrator describes his first meal and find the words that suggest how special it is ('wonderful', 'savouring', 'precious', 'sweeter', 'delicious').

- Ask the children: *Why is Michael excited about the possibility of making fire? Why does he need fire? How many reasons can they come up with?*

- Ask: *Who do you think the man is? Why has he put out the fire?*

Ask the children, whenever appropriate, to revisit the text to exemplify/support their answers.

Encourage the children to read aloud back to the group when referring back to the text – praise clear, confident and expressive reading.

## Before the next session

Ask the children to read Chapter 5 up to 'The thought didn't bear dwelling on'. As they read, ask them to consider the new character who appears. What is their opinion of him? How might his appearance affect Michael and what happens to him?

## ASSESSMENT OPPORTUNITIES

The following bank of question prompts provides a quick and easy means of monitoring the children's comprehension skills and understanding of the text. The children's answers to a question must be supported by evidence from the text.

### Understanding

- What are Michael's thoughts as he floats alone in the ocean?
- What helps Michael to stay afloat in the water?
- Where does Michael go to see further out to sea?
- Is the sun low or high in the sky by the time Michael reaches the beach on the other side of the island?
- What helps to calm the panic that comes over Michael in his first hours on the island?
- List the 'cruel' realities Michael is faced with on the island.

### Inferences

- Do you think Michael is dreaming that he is being rescued from the seawater? Why do you think this?
- Why do you think the howling of the gibbons is not immediately menacing to Michael?
- Is Michael excited about being on the island despite feeling anxious? How do you know?
- Explain why Michael is particularly desperate to make a fire.
- Why do you think the stranger who leaves food and water for Michael and the dog does not introduce himself?
- What further dangers do you think are ahead for Michael and Stella Artois? Why do you think this?

### Predicting

- Do you think Michael will find out who the man is? How will their interaction develop?
- How likely do you think it is that Michael's parents will soon return to find him?

### Main ideas

- What do you think has been the worst of Michael's experiences on the island so far? Explain why you say this.
- Why is Stella Artois so important to Michael?

### Language, structure and presentation

- What does the narrator compare the island to? What does he mean by this?
- The forest becomes 'impenetrable'. Explain what is meant by 'impenetrable' here.
- Michael finds 'Thin strips of translucent white fish'. Suggest another word with the same meaning as 'translucent'.

# SESSION 4: KENSUKE

## SESSION AIMS

Begin to consider the character of Kensuke and his attitude towards Michael.

## BEFORE THE SESSION

The children should have read Chapter 5 up to 'The thought didn't bear dwelling on.'

## READ

- Invite the children to share their opinions on the new character of Kensuke from what they have read so far. How do they think his appearance might impact on Michael?

- Why do the children think Stella Artois greets the old man 'like a long lost friend'? Have they met before? Michael feels he has seen the old man before. Ask the children: *Do you have any idea how that could be?*

- Do the children know the meaning of the words 'diminutive' and 'gesticulating'? Can they work this out from the context?

- Ask the children: *What clues about his appearance lets Michael know that the person he meets is an old man?*

- Ask: *What surprised Michael about Stella Artois' attitude to the old man? How did Michael feel about it?*

- Can the children see a link between the old man's writing in the sand map and the unusual contents list at the front of the book?

- Can the children find any explanation for the old man helping Michael but dividing the island between them?

### During reading

- Ask the children to read independently to the end of Chapter 5, considering the relationship between Michael and Kensuke.

- If your school uses reading journals then the children should be encouraged to make notes as they read and consider each question.

- Move around the group and 'tune in' to hear individuals read aloud. Encourage and praise good expression.

## REVISIT AND RESPOND

Use the following discussion points to help the children think about what they have read in more depth.

**Note:** Since there are only 20 minutes for each session, you are advised to focus on only one or two of the elements that are listed below.

- Ask the children: *How does Michael feel when he first meets the stranger?* (He is very confused – understandably.)

- Do the children think it is the old man who is leaving the food? Why is he helping Michael? Are the children able to come up with any explanations for the old man's behaviour? Draw their attention to 'None of it made any sense at all, unless he was out of his head and completely mad.'

- Ask the children:
  - What questions did Michael have about Kensuke? Would the children have any other questions?
  - What made Michael confident that he could survive on the island? How would you feel if you were Michael?
  - What did Michael think was the deal with Kensuke? What did Michael think he had to do in order to be kept fed and watered?
  - What clues are there to suggest that Kensuke had been on the island a long time?

- Michael said he was disappointed and dejected but not despondent. Invite the children to explain the difference between these.

Ask the children, whenever appropriate, to revisit the text to exemplify/support their answers.

Encourage the children to read aloud back to the group when referring back to the text – praise clear, confident and expressive reading.

## Before the next session

Ask the children to read Chapter 6, considering the developing relationship between Michael and Kensuke.

## ASSESSMENT OPPORTUNITIES

The following bank of question prompts provides a quick and easy means of monitoring the children's comprehension skills and understanding of the text. The children's answers to a question must be supported by evidence from the text.

### Understanding

- How does Stella Artois greet the old man?
- What kept Michael awake at night on the island?
- What was Michael's 'fireglass'?
- How did Michael know where his part of the island ended and Kensuke's began?
- What was often wrong with the coconuts that Michael found?
- Why did Michael not climb the trees to get coconuts?
- Why could Michael not catch the fish he saw in the shallows?
- What did Michael see accompanying the old man when he went spearfishing?
- Which fruit did Michael find irresistible?
- How did Michael get some relief from the mosquito bites and sores?
- What did Kensuke leave for Michael that helped him to sleep at night? What does this tell you about him?
- What was the best part of the day for Michael and Stella Artois?
- What did Michael use to make his sunhat?

### Inferences

- Why was it important for Michael to build a large fire?
- The old man is against Michael lighting a fire on the island. Why do you think this is?
- Why did Michael not want to confront the old man?
- What, apart from Kensuke's rules, prevented Michael from going into his side of the island?

- Why do you think Michael and the old man's relationship is particularly difficult?
- Why do you think the old man provides food and water for Michael and his dog when he doesn't seem to want them on the island?
- Do you think there might be anyone else on the island? Why?
- How do you think Michael felt when he saw the supertanker on the horizon?

### Predicting

- Will Kensuke stay angry with Michael and apart from him, or begin to make friends? Explain your reasons.

### Main ideas

- Explain what you have learned about Kensuke so far.
- 'He said not a word, but set about stamping out my embryo fire' (page 95). How do you think the author wants you to feel here? Explain your reasons.
- Do you identify with the old man's point of view at any time? Explain why you say this.

### Language, structure and presentation

- Michael feels that the old man is banishing him to the other side of the island as if he were a 'leper'. What do you think he means when he says this?

# SESSION 5: ABUNAI!

## SESSION AIMS

Identify with the two main characters' differing points of view.

## BEFORE THE SESSION

The children should have read Chapter 6.

## READ

- Discuss Michael's thoughts and emotions at seeing the supertanker and watching it slowly disappear. Ask the children: *Why do you think the slowness is an important part of this event?*

- Michael thinks Kensuke is effectively keeping him prisoner on the island by not letting him build a fire. Ask: *Why do you think Kensuke does this when he wants to keep separate from Michael?*

- Ask: *What was Michael's reaction to Kensuke telling him not to swim? Why do you think Michael feels like this?*

- Kensuke says sorry after destroying Michael's beacon, but now Michael has lost a chance of escape. Ask: *Why does he say sorry? What are his motives?*

- Ask the children: *What reason do you think Kensuke had for forbidding Michael from swimming?*

### During reading

- Ask the children to read Chapter 7 independently, noting the ways in which the relationship between Michael and Kensuke develops.

- If your school uses reading journals then the children should be encouraged to make notes as they read and consider each question.

- Move around the group and 'tune in' to hear individuals read aloud. Encourage and praise good expression.

## REVISIT AND RESPOND

Use the following discussion points to help the children think about what they have read in more depth.

**Note:** Since there are only 20 minutes for each session, you are advised to focus on only one or two of the elements that are listed below.

- Look for clues in the text to work out how many days Michael was ill.

- Michael says 'There were a thousand mysteries, a thousand things I wanted to know.' In this part of the book there are a lot of unanswered questions. Encourage the children to think about the mysteries and record the questions that Michael must want to ask Kensuke.

- Ask the children: *Why is painting so important in this part of the story?* Explore with them how, when Michael is recovering in the cave, he watches Kensuke paint but says that Kensuke 'never showed me what he had done.' After some time has passed, Kensuke gives Michael a picture and after that shows him 'all the paintings he did.' Eventually the old man invites Michael to paint with him. Point out that this suggests they are growing to trust and like one another.

- When Michael recovers he sounds very happy with his life with Kensuke. He says that although he thinks about his parents he no longer misses them. What do the children think about this? Can they imagine being Michael – can they understand how he feels? Ask them: *Would you enjoy Michael's life on the island? How long has Michael been on the island?*

- Were the children surprised to read that Kensuke had a fire when he had told Michael not to have one? Can they explain this difference?

Ask the children, whenever appropriate, to revisit the text to exemplify/support their answers.

Encourage the children to read aloud back to the group when referring back to the text – praise clear, confident and expressive reading.

## Before the next session

Invite the children to make a list of questions they would want to ask Kensuke.

## ASSESSMENT OPPORTUNITIES

The following bank of question prompts provides a quick and easy means of monitoring the children's comprehension skills and understanding of the text. The children's answers to a question must be supported by evidence from the text.

### Understanding

- Why did the smell of vinegar remind Michael of home?
- How had the jellyfish sting affected Michael?
- What things did Kensuke do to help Michael when he was ill?
- What made Kensuke smile for the first time since Michael had met him?
- In what ways was Kensuke's cave different from Michael's?
- What did Kensuke paint on?
- What questions did Michael want to ask Kensuke?
- Where was Kensuke from?
- How did Kensuke call the orang-utans?
- List the things Kensuke taught Michael.
- What did Kensuke use to make a paintbrush?
- What did Michael teach Kensuke, at his request?
- List the activities that are a part of daily life in Kensuke's cave.

### Inferences

- Why do you think Michael was so pleased to see his football? Why is it so important to him?
- When Kensuke is nursing him, Michael describes how 'the silence between us said more than any words'. Do you think this is an important moment in the story? Explain why.
- Why do you think Kensuke often washed away his paintings?
- Why were all Kensuke's paintings black and white?
- Why and how do you think Kensuke developed such a close relationship with the orang-utans?

- How do you think Michael felt when Kensuke showed him his lost football?
- How do you think Michael feels about Kensuke after sharing his home with him for several months?

### Predicting

- Now that they are friends, what do you think will happen next? Will Michael settle happily on the island, or something else?

### Main ideas

- Why do you think Kensuke's attitude to Michael changed so dramatically?
- Think about what you know of Kensuke from when he first appeared in the story. Have you changed the way you feel about Kensuke? If so, at which point in the story did you begin to feel differently about Kensuke, and why?
- Explain how you think Michael feels when he is telling Kensuke all about home in England.
- What do you think Kensuke might want to know about Michael?

### Language, structure and presentation

- What is the meaning of the word 'rudimentary'?

### Themes and conventions

- We have seen how, from an unpromising start, a close friendship has developed. Why do you think it took a near disaster for this to happen?
- Would you enjoy Michael's life on the island? Explain your reasons.

# ▼ SESSION 6: EVERYONE DEAD IN NAGASAKI

## SESSION AIMS

Learn more about the character of Kensuke.

## BEFORE THE SESSION

The children should have prepared a list of questions for Kensuke.

## READ

- Begin by inviting the children to share the questions they prepared to ask Kensuke. Put yourself or one of the children in the hot seat to answer the questions. Afterwards, discuss the impact of knowing very little about Kensuke for so much of the story. How do the children think the story would be different if Kensuke had befriended Michael immediately? (For example, there would be little tension and a sense of mystery would have been lost.)

- Ask the children: *Do you agree that the way in which Kensuke changes in his attitude to Michael makes the story more interesting?*

- Ask the children to read Chapter 8 independently.

### During reading

- Encourage the children to think about the information and questions that arise for them as they read.

- If your school uses reading journals then the children should be encouraged to make notes as they read and consider each question.

- Move around the group and 'tune in' to hear individuals read aloud. Encourage and praise good expression.

## REVISIT AND RESPOND

Use the following discussion points to help the children think about what they have read in more depth.

**Note:** Since there are only 20 minutes for each session, you are advised to focus on only one or two of the elements that are listed below.

- Kensuke could speak little English when he lived in London – but he learns English quickly from Michael. Ask the children: *Why do you think the author has done this? Is it important to the plot?*

- Ask: *How does the author let us know that Michael feels guilty about sending a message in a bottle? Why do you think he feels like this?*

- Do the children know anything about Nagasaki? Ask them to skim over the text from 'Now I tell you everything, Micasan'. What do the children think about Kensuke's decisions? Can they understand why he was afraid? Tell the children that Japanese soldiers saw surrender as dishonourable.

- Look back over the story – so many questions are answered and truths revealed in this chapter. Did the children guess at any of the answers and connections?

- Ask the children: *When Kensuke finds the bottle with Michael's note in it, how could he read it?* (He apparently doesn't speak much English.) *Does Kensuke need to read the message to understand what has happened?* How do the children feel at the end of this chapter? Explore with them what they think will happen next.

- If Michael had found the outrigger earlier, do the children think he would have tried to use it to escape from the island? Ask them: *Why was it important to the story that Michael didn't escape?*

Ask the children, whenever appropriate, to revisit the text to exemplify/support their answers.

Encourage the children to read aloud back to the group when referring back to the text – praise clear, confident and expressive reading.

## Before the next session

Invite the children to carry out some research into Japan's involvement in the Second World War, and in particular the bombing of Hiroshima and Nagasaki. Can they find out what Nagasaki is like today?

## ASSESSMENT OPPORTUNITIES

The following bank of question prompts provides a quick and easy means of monitoring the children's comprehension skills and understanding of the text. The children's answers to a question must be supported by evidence from the text.

### Understanding

- How does Kensuke row his heavy outrigger?
- What was Kensuke's profession before the war?
- Where did Kensuke study his profession?
- Why had Kensuke joined the navy?
- In what way did Kensuke say war was like football?
- How had Kensuke come to be on the island?
- What had happened to Kensuke's hometown of Nagasaki? How did he know?
- Why had the 'killer men' come to the island? What did their presence do to reinforce Kensuke's mistrust of people?
- What reason does Kensuke give for not wanting Michael to have a fire?
- For how many years had Kensuke been on the island?
- How did Stella Artois give Michael away?

### Inferences

- How had Kensuke learned to survive on the island?
- Why was it important for Kensuke not to surrender to the Americans?
- How would Kensuke's life on the island have been different if he hadn't had all the things he took from the ship?
- Why do you think Michael hadn't realised it had been Kensuke who had rescued him from the sea?
- Apart from Michael, had Kensuke rescued anyone else on the island? How do you know?

- Does Kensuke feel protective over Michael? Explain your thinking.
- Is Michael feeling homesick? How do you know?

### Predicting

- How do you think Kensuke will react to the message Michael has sent in the bottle? Why do you think this?

### Main ideas

- Why was Kensuke content to remain on the island?
- Why do you think Kensuke helped Michael when he was so angry with people and wanted to be alone? Why didn't he let him die?
- Michael wanted to leave the island to find his parents, but also to stay with Kensuke. Explain his emotions in this predicament.
- Why do you think Michael didn't tell Kensuke how he felt and about sending his message in a bottle?

### Language, structure and presentation

- When Kensuke speaks in English after learning from Michael, how can we tell he is using it as a second language? What types of words are missing when Kensuke speaks?
- 'Kensuke dispatched it quickly, a sharp blow to the back of the neck…' Explain what you think 'dispatched' means here.
- Explain what Michael means when he uses the word 'betrayal' when he is thinking about sending a message in the bottle.
- How do you think Michael is feeling when he talks of the 'entire forest cackling and screeching its condemnation'.

# ▼ SESSION 7: THE NIGHT OF THE TURTLES

## SESSION AIMS

Investigate the changing relationship between Kensuke and Michael.

## BEFORE THE SESSION

The children should have carried out some research into Japan's role in the Second World War and the city of Nagasaki.

## READ

- Invite the children to share what they have found out about Japan's involvement in the Second World War, and about the bombing of both Hiroshima and Nagasaki. What have they discovered about the city today?

- Based on what they have learned about Nagasaki and the war, invite the children to discuss Kensuke's attitude to the Americans and his reluctance to return to his home. Ask them: *What would you do in Kensuke's situation?*

**During reading**

- Ask the children to read Chapter 9 in this session, keeping in mind Kensuke's reaction to finding Michael's note.

- If your school uses reading journals then the children should be encouraged to make notes as they read and consider each question.

- Move around the group and 'tune in' to hear individuals read aloud. Encourage and praise good expression.

## REVISIT AND RESPOND

Use the following discussion points to help the children think about what they have read in more depth.

**Note:** Since there are only 20 minutes for each session, you are advised to focus on only one or two of the elements that are listed below.

- Invite the children to discuss how Michael and Kensuke's relationship changed after Stella Artois brought back the message in the bottle. Do the children understand Kensuke's reaction? What do they think Kensuke was thinking and feeling?

- Look at the language the author uses to describe how Kensuke feels and behaves ('He had closed in on himself'; 'The warmth had gone'; 'distance'; 'lost friendship'; 'treachery'). Ask: *Is this a reasonable way for an adult to treat a child who is missing his parents? Is the author's portrayal of the relationship between Kensuke and Michael realistic?* Explore with the children how Kensuke's experiences during the war and on the island might explain why he behaves in this way.

- Michael says 'I painted the best picture of the world outside I could'. Ask the children to think about what they would say to persuade Kensuke to come with them. Remember how long Kensuke has been on the island.

- Kensuke really wants to know about Japan, but Michael doesn't know very much. How much could the children tell Kensuke about Japan?

Ask the children, whenever appropriate, to revisit the text to exemplify/support their answers.

Encourage the children to read aloud back to the group when referring back to the text – praise clear, confident and expressive reading.

## ASSESSMENT OPPORTUNITIES

The following bank of question prompts provides a quick and easy means of monitoring the children's comprehension skills and understanding of the text. The children's answers to a question must be supported by evidence from the text.

### Understanding

- Why did Tomodachi, the orang-utan, keep coming to the mouth of the cave?
- What do Kensuke and Michael use the firewood at the back of the cave for?
- What was Michael careful not to speak to Kensuke about?
- How did Michael try to persuade Kensuke to leave the island?
- Why did Kensuke decide to help Michael build a beacon on the hilltop?
- Where did Kensuke seem happiest to talk to Michael? Why do you think this?
- How old was Kensuke? How old would his son have been?
- Why did Michael not tell Kensuke about the bad things that had happened in the world?
- What did Michael and Kensuke do to help the newly hatched turtles?
- Why did cherry trees remind Kensuke of his twin sister?
- What lesson did the baby turtles teach Kensuke?

### Inferences

- In what way did Tomodachi losing her baby make Kensuke think again about Michael's situation?
- How do you think Michael felt when Kensuke told him that he felt as though they were father and son?
- Explain how Kensuke's behaviour affects Michael.
- What happens to improve the relationship between the old man and the boy?

- Why did Kensuke want to know about modern Japan?
- Why did Kensuke assume his wife and son were dead?
- Why did Michael have mixed feelings about sighting a ship and potentially leaving the island?
- How do you think Michael felt when Kensuke told him he would go with him when a boat came?
- Why do you think Kensuke was happy with his life on the island?
- How do you know that Michael, Kensuke and Stella Artois all enjoyed the football game?
- What new technology did Michael find difficult to explain to Kensuke?

### Predicting

- In the final chapter, do you think a boat will come?
- If a boat does come, do you think Kensuke will do as he says and go with Michael or not? Explain your reasons.

### Main ideas

- Why did Kensuke not want to return to Japan?
- What more do we learn about Kensuke's character in this chapter?
- Explain why Kensuke decides to put Michael's wishes to leave the island before his own wishes to keep Michael as his companion.

### Language, structure and presentation

- Give an example from the text that demonstrates that Kensuke has a sense of humour.
- 'I always scanned the horizon both in hope and in trepidation.' What does Michael mean by 'trepidation' here?
- Kensuke and Michael kept their 'vigil' all night long as the infant turtles made a run for the sea. Explain the meaning of 'vigil' here.

# ▼ SESSION 8: THE END OF THE STORY

## SESSION AIMS

Consider points of view and underlying themes of the story.
Consider character motivation and how it affects their actions.

## BEFORE THE SESSION

The children should have prepared questions they would like to ask Kensuke and Michael.

## READ

- Invite the children to ask some of the questions they have prepared, with members of the group answering in role.
- Did the children come up with similar questions, or were some of them very different? Was there a theme to their questions?

### During reading

- Ask the children to read the final chapter and the postscript. As they read, ask them to think about how Michael and Kensuke's friendship has developed and how they think each would feel at the end of the story.
- If your school uses reading journals then the children should be encouraged to make notes as they read and consider each question.
- Move around the group and 'tune in' to hear individuals read aloud. Encourage and praise good expression.

## REVISIT AND RESPOND

Use the following discussion points to help the children think about what they have read in more depth.

**Note:** Since there are only 20 minutes for each session, you are advised to focus on only one or two of the elements that are listed below.

- The rain kept Michael and Kensuke in the cave for several days. Kensuke said the rain was a 'very good thing'. Did Michael think this? Discuss the children's thoughts about the situation, when Michael and Kensuke were both waiting to light the beacon if they saw a ship. Ask: *What difference did the rain make to lighting the beacon?*
- As they wait for rescue, Kensuke continues to live as he had always done, as though it didn't matter when rescue came. He had become very good at waiting. Invite the children to explain why this was the case. Why was Michael less good at waiting?
- Ask the children: *What effect did the shooting of the gibbons have on Kensuke? Why did it affect him so much?*
- Invite the children to describe the feelings that Michael and Kensuke would have when they saw the boat coming towards the island. Ask: *Would they each feel the same?*
- Ask: *Should Kensuke have left the island with Michael? Would this have been a happier ending?* Invite the children to imagine that Kensuke went back to Japan and found Michiya; ask them to tell Kensuke's story in dialogue, as he might have told it to his son.
- The narrator of the story is called Michael and so is the author of the book. Which Michael do the children think the letter was sent to? Ask them: *Does it make you think that perhaps the events in the story were true? Do you think Michiya would want to go back to the island to let Kensuke know he was alive? Do you think Kensuke would still be alive by then?*

Ask the children, whenever appropriate, to revisit the text to exemplify/support their answers.

Encourage the children to read aloud back to the group when referring back to the text – praise clear, confident and expressive reading.

## ASSESSMENT OPPORTUNITIES

The following bank of question prompts provides a quick and easy means of monitoring the children's comprehension skills and understanding of the text. The children's answers to a question must be supported by evidence from the text.

### Understanding

- Why did Kensuke and Michael have to stay in the cave for several days?
- What was the difference between rain on the island and rain that Michael was used to at home?
- What did Kensuke make with most of the berries they gathered?
- Why did Michael and Kensuke have to stop painting?
- What was unusual about the faces that Kensuke painted?
- What was the subject of the first of Michael's paintings that Kensuke kept?
- How did Kensuke get the stolen binoculars back from Kikanbo?
- What made Stella Artois growl and bark when she was on top of the hill?
- Why did Kensuke not want to attract the attention of the junk?
- How did Kensuke attract the orang-utans?
- Why did Kensuke want to get the orang-utans into the cave?
- Which story was Michael reminded of when he and Kensuke were leading the orang-utans to the cave?
- Which orang-utan was missing?
- Why did Kensuke build a bamboo cage in his cave?
- What were Kensuke and Michael doing when Kensuke sighted the boat?

### Inferences

- Do you think Kensuke was right to keep hidden from the men with the guns? Why?

- What did Kensuke and Michael think had happened to Kikanbo?
- How do we know the gibbons never came to Kensuke's singing?
- How do you think Michael would feel at leaving Kensuke behind? Explain your reasons.
- How would Michael's parents feel when they found him?
- How have we always known that Michael escaped from the island?

### Predicting

- Do you think Michael would ever return to the island? What might he find there?
- How do you think Michael would find life after living on the island? How might it have changed him?

### Main ideas

- What reasons did Kensuke have for staying on the island?
- What three things did Kensuke ask Michael to promise?
- Why did Kensuke want Michael to keep his story a secret?
- What could Michael have said to convince his parents that he had survived alone on the island, if he was to keep his promise to Kensuke? How would he have to change his story?

### Language, structure and presentation

- Kensuke was 'stoical' about the prolonged rain. What does this mean?
- What is your opinion of the end of the story?

### Themes and conventions

- How well do you think the author gets across the idea of friendship between a young and an old person?

- One of the things we see from the way Kensuke and Michael live on the island is that they survive well on what they find. What message does this give to us about how we live our lives?

# ▼ SESSION 1: STORIES

## SESSION AIMS

Ask questions to improve understanding of the text.

## BEFORE THE SESSION

The children should have read Chapter 2 prior to the session.

## READ

- Ask the children to talk to a partner about what has happened in the story so far and to scan Chapter 2 independently or with a partner to remind themselves of recent events.
- Involve the children in a brief group discussion. Ask them:
  - What is 'the only bright thing' in the grandparents' lives?
  - Who seems to know most about Mr Willy Wonka?
  - Whose story does Grandpa Joe agree to tell Charlie?
- Ask the children: *How does Grandpa Joe know so much about Mr Wonka?* (This question focuses on story information that the reader is left wanting to ask questions about.) Ask the children to read Chapter 3 independently, keeping this question in mind.

### During reading

- Ask the children to think about the information and the questions that arise for them as they read.
- If your school uses reading journals then the children should be encouraged to make notes as they read and consider each question.
- Move around the group and 'tune in' to hear individuals read aloud. Encourage and praise good expression.

## REVISIT AND RESPOND

Use the following discussion points to help the children think about what they have read in more depth.

**Note:** Since there are only 20 minutes for each session, you are advised to focus on only one or two of the elements that are listed below.

- Check how many characters have been introduced by the end of Chapter 2. Which character(s) do the children think will be the most important? Why? What do they know about the characters so far? What questions do they have that the author has not yet answered? Encourage the children to share questions and answers. (You could link this to Activity 1 on page 25 of *Read and Respond Charlie and the Chocolate Factory*.)
- Ask the children to find examples of important questions that Charlie asks the grandparents about Mr Wonka and the chocolate factory. Encourage the children to put themselves in Charlie's place. What questions would they ask the grandparents?
- Examine Charlie's relationship with the grandparents. Ask the children: *How do the grandparents feel about Charlie? How does Charlie feel about spending time with them?* Do the children spend enjoyable time with older people? Share experiences.
- Let the children re-read the final paragraphs of Chapter 3. Do they think the grandparents are being serious? Is Grandpa Joe probably telling the truth? Could he be just a skilful storyteller?
- Focus on examples in Chapter 3 of Charlie's concentration and involvement in the Indian Prince story. Create a group list of all the times he shows this interest and belief. What physical details are there? Are there times when Charlie doubts the story's truth? If so, how is this shown?
- Discuss Grandpa Joe's storytelling skills. Comment on the detailed description, the inclusion of dialogue, emphasis, and pausing at exciting points. Encourage the children to support these points with examples.

- Consider the other grandparents' reactions to listening to Grandpa Joe. Do they enjoy listening while he does most of the talking? Do they think he has more energy than they have? You could use a hot-seat activity (as in Activity 1 on page 32 of *Read and Respond Charlie and the Chocolate Factory*) to question them about their feelings.

Ask the children, whenever appropriate, to revisit the text to exemplify/support their answers.

Encourage the children to read aloud back to the group when referring back to the text – praise clear, confident and expressive reading.

## ASSESSMENT OPPORTUNITIES

The following bank of question prompts provides a quick and easy means of monitoring the children's comprehension skills and understanding of the text. The children's answers to a question must be supported by evidence from the text.

### Understanding

- What is so unusual about Mr Wonka's chocolate ice cream?
- Who encourages Grandpa Joe to tell Charlie the story of Prince Pondicherry?
- How does Prince Pondicherry make contact with Mr Wonka?
- What request does the Prince make?
- What convinces Charlie that the story about Prince Pondicherry is true?
- What is mysterious about Mr Wonka's factory?

### Inferences

- How does Charlie's presence change the grandparents?
- Which grandparent character is painted most vividly? How?
- Why could the reader find Grandpa Joe a more interesting character than the other three old people?
- Do you think the author uses dialogue effectively in Chapter 3? How does it enhance the story?
- What impression of Mr Willy Wonka does Charlie gain from the grandparents, particularly Grandpa Joe?

### Predicting

- What do you think will happen in Chapter 4?

### Main ideas

- How does the author create an air of mystery around Mr Wonka and his chocolate factory? Are the children surprised by how often Mr Wonka and his chocolate factory are mentioned?
- Why have we still not 'met' Mr Wonka by the end of Chapter 3? What is the effect of just hearing about him through another character?

### Language, structure and presentation

- How did the author decide where to end chapters? Do chapters end at interesting points?
- Why does Charlie ask the other grandparents if Grandpa Joe is 'pulling my leg'? What does the expression mean?
- Find a synonym for 'clevernesses' near the end of Chapter 3.
- What words does the author use in Chapter 2 to emphasise the age of the grandparents?

# ▼ SESSION 2: SPECIAL WORDS

## SESSION AIMS

Discuss and explain the meaning of words in context.

## BEFORE THE SESSION

The children should have read Chapter 5 prior to the session.

## READ

- Ask the children to talk to a partner about what has happened in the story so far and to scan Chapters 4 and 5 independently to remind themselves of recent events.
- Involve the children in a brief group discussion. Ask them:
  - How many Golden Tickets are there?
  - Why are the Golden Tickets of particular interest to children?
  - What will be the winners' special present at the end of their tour?
- Ask the children: *What does Grandpa Joe mean when he talks of the factory workers as 'one of the great mysteries of the chocolate-making world'?* (This question focuses on the reader understanding the author's words.) Ask the children to read Chapter 6 independently, keeping this question in mind.

### During reading

- Ask the children to think about the information and the questions that arise for them as they read.
- If your school uses reading journals then the children should be encouraged to make notes as they read and consider each question.
- Move around the group and 'tune in' to hear individuals read aloud. Encourage and praise good expression.

## REVISIT AND RESPOND

Use the following discussion points to help the children think about what they have read in more depth.

**Note:** Since there are only 20 minutes for each session, you are advised to focus on only one or two of the elements that are listed below.

- Investigate Mr Wonka's language in his newspaper notice at the beginning of Chapter 5. How many times are the words 'five' and 'Golden Tickets' used? What effect does the repetition have? Is it an effective device? Let the group collaborate on a new notice for Mr Wonka to have published.
- Explore the reaction of the listening grandparents to Mr Wonka's published announcement in Chapter 5. Ask the children to identify positive and negative words that the grandparents use. Create two lists. Which reaction prevails: positive or negative?
- Consider the names 'Augustus Gloop' and 'Veruca Salt'. How do the children react when the names are said aloud? Share reactions. Do they find the name 'Veruca' strange? What does the word mean? Encourage the group to exchange views about Dahl's intention in his choice of names. Is he making fun of the two children?
- Debate the morality of Mr Salt's behaviour. Is there anything wrong with buying so many Wonka bars? Does he treat his staff fairly? Encourage the children to listen to one another's views before reaching a majority decision.
- Investigate the information about Veruca's and Augustus's parents in Chapter 6. What information has the author included in the text? What important words does he use?
- Debate Mrs Gloop's attitude to her son. Do the children think there is truth in what she says about nourishment? Ask them to put themselves in her position. What attitude would they have to Augustus's love of chocolate? Let the group share views.

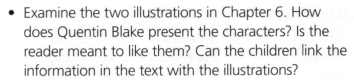

• Examine the two illustrations in Chapter 6. How does Quentin Blake present the characters? Is the reader meant to like them? Can the children link the information in the text with the illustrations?

Ask the children, whenever appropriate, to revisit the text to exemplify/support their answers.

Encourage the children to read aloud back to the group when referring back to the text – praise clear, confident and expressive reading.

## ASSESSMENT OPPORTUNITIES

The following bank of question prompts provides a quick and easy means of monitoring the children's comprehension skills and understanding of the text. The children's answers to a question must be supported by evidence from the text.

### Understanding

• Who finds the first Golden Ticket?
• What helps Augustus win a Golden Ticket?
• What does Professor Foulbody invent?
• Why does the mechanical arm not find a winning ticket?
• Why is Mr Salt's job useful for him at this time?
• What does Charlie expect for his birthday?

### Inferences

• Why does Grandpa George say that 'there isn't a hope' of Charlie winning a Golden Ticket?
• Why does Charlie think that Mr Salt did not play it 'quite fair'?
• Why is 'Salt' an appropriate name for the author to give this character?
• What is lucky for Charlie about his birthday this year?
• Why does Uncle Joe want to see Charlie take the wrapper off his birthday bar of chocolate?

### Predicting

• What do you think will happen in Chapter 7?
• Will Charlie win a Golden Ticket? How could this happen?

### Main ideas

• Is the public excited about Mr Wonka's competition? What words or happenings in Chapter 6 make you think this?
• Consider the two new children presented in this part of the book. Are they attractive characters? Why/why not? Find evidence in the text to support your views.

### Language, structure and presentation

• Consider the use of large capital letters and bold font for some words in Chapter 4. Why do you think the author uses this device?
• What does the name 'Charlotte Russe' have to do with sweet food?
• What does the author mean when he describes Mr Wonka in Chapter 5 as a 'confectionery genius'?
• What do you notice about the language used in Mr Wonka's announcement in Chapter 5? How does the announcement's language, structure and presentation differ from the rest of the chapter?

### Themes and conventions

• Is the author emphasising the difference between Charlie and children who are given everything they want? If so, how is this done?

# ▼ SESSION 3: CHANGE

## SESSION AIMS

Consider character attitudes, feelings and thoughts and reader response.

## BEFORE THE SESSION

The children should have read Chapter 9 prior to the session.

## READ

- Ask the children to talk to a partner about what has happened in the story so far and to scan Chapter 9 independently to remind themselves of recent events.

- Involve the children in a brief group discussion. Ask:
  - What new characteristics does Grandpa Joe reveal in Chapter 9?
  - Do you think Uncle Joe is wrong to hide and then waste sixpence?
  - Why has the illustrator not added pictures to Chapter 9?

- Ask the children: *Are you surprised that Grandpa Joe and Charlie think selfishly of their own pleasure when they secretly buy chocolate?* (This question focuses on a central character's feelings and behaviour.) Ask the children to read Chapter 10, keeping this question in mind.

### During reading

- Ask the children to think about the information and the questions that arise for them as they read.

- If your school uses reading journals then the children should be encouraged to make notes as they read and consider each question.

- Move around the group and 'tune in' to hear individuals read aloud. Encourage and praise good expression.

## REVISIT AND RESPOND

Use the following discussion points to help the children think about what they have read in more depth.

**Note:** Since there are only 20 minutes for each session, you are advised to focus on only one or two of the elements that are listed below.

- New aspects of Grandpa Joe's character are evident in Chapter 9. Ask the children which aspects of his character they find surprising or particularly interesting. What does he do or say to reveal the character traits? The children should refer to the text to support their views.

- Compare the atmosphere and mood of Chapter 10 to that of Chapter 9. How are they different? Ask the children: *What effect does Chapter 9 have on your attitude to Charlie and his family's way of life? Do you feel differently when you read Chapter 10? Do the family members change?*

- Encourage the children to think about how they would feel if they were one of the Bucket family, struggling to cope with the weather and the shortage of food. Would they worry about themselves or others in the family? What would they try to do? Ask the children to express their feelings in role.

- Explore Mrs Bucket's attitude to the problem of feeding the family. How does she cope? How does she try to make sure that Charlie, a growing boy, stays healthy? Do other family member notice her actions?

- Focus on the winter weather in Chapter 10. Create a group list of similes and descriptive words and phrases used to describe the weather. How does the weather affect the family?

- Ask the children to work as a group to create a character profile of Mr Bucket. What information is there about him in Chapter 10? What actions reveal his personality? You could use a hot-seat activity and progress to examining the other characters (for example, see Activity 1 on page 32 of *Read and Respond Charlie and the Chocolate Factory*).

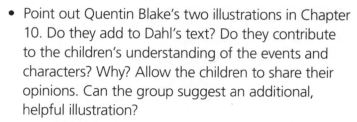

• Point out Quentin Blake's two illustrations in Chapter 10. Do they add to Dahl's text? Do they contribute to the children's understanding of the events and characters? Why? Allow the children to share their opinions. Can the group suggest an additional, helpful illustration?

Ask the children, whenever appropriate, to revisit the text to exemplify/support their answers.

Encourage the children to read aloud back to the group when referring back to the text – praise clear, confident and expressive reading.

## ASSESSMENT OPPORTUNITIES

The following bank of question prompts provides a quick and easy means of monitoring the children's comprehension skills and understanding of the text. The children's answers to a question must be supported by evidence from the text.

### Understanding
• What has Grandpa Joe kept hidden?
• What does Grandpa Joe ask Charlie to do with the sixpence?
• Why does Mr Bucket dig a deep path?
• Why do the Buckets' meals become thinner?
• Which factory closes?
• Why is the toothpaste factory important to the Bucket family?

### Inferences
• Why do Grandpa Joe and Charlie laugh when a Golden Ticket is not in their chocolate?
• Is Charlie excited when he sees the snow falling?
• Why does the family not talk about the Golden Tickets anymore?
• Why does Charlies look around before he decides that the fifty-pence piece is his?
• Why do other people in the illustration in Chapter 10 look more comfortable than Charlie?

### Predicting
• What might happen in Chapter 11? Will Charlie buy himself a bar of chocolate?

### Main ideas
• What new idea is introduced into the story in Chapter 10? Did Charlie seem a happier boy earlier in the story?
• Why does the author not include any dialogue in Chapter 10? What effect does this have on the reader's attitude to Charlie and his family's state of mind?

### Language, structure and presentation
• Why does the illustrator choose to put rather gloomy pictures in Chapter 10? What is the effect on the reader?
• What is a 'sixpence'?
• How does Charlie's behaviour change during Chapter 10? What is Charlie trying to avoid?
• Why does the author write 'FOOD' in capital letters near the end of Chapter 10?

### Themes and conventions
• How does the author explore the experience of being poor? How does he contrast this with the experience of being wealthy/not living in poverty?

# ▼ SESSION 4: GAINING ENTRY

## SESSION AIMS

Make sense of the text.

## BEFORE THE SESSION

The children should have read Chapter 13 prior to the session.

## READ

- Ask the children to talk to a partner about what has happened in the story so far and to scan Chapters 12 and 13 independently, to remind themselves of recent events.

- Involve the children in a brief group discussion. Ask them:

  - Who is chosen to accompany Charlie to the factory?

  - Why does Charlie hold Grandpa Joe's hand tightly when they wait outside the factory?

  - How are the other waiting groups different from Charlie and Grandpa Joe?

- Ask the children: *Are Mr and Mrs Bucket not interested in going to the chocolate factory?* (This question focuses on understanding details in the story.) Then ask them to read Chapter 14 independently, keeping this type of detailed question in mind.

### During reading

- Ask the children to think about the information and the questions that arise for them as they read.

- If your school uses reading journals then the children should be encouraged to make notes as they read and consider each question.

- Move around the group and 'tune in' to hear individuals read aloud. Encourage and praise good expression.

## REVISIT AND RESPOND

Use the following discussion points to help the children think about what they have read in more depth.

**Note:** Since there are only 20 minutes for each session, you are advised to focus on only one or two of the elements that are listed below.

- Examine the effect of Charlie's win on Grandpa Joe in Chapter 12. How does he change? What is amazing about his behaviour? Do the children think that he becomes a more interesting character?

- Use Chapter 12 to investigate the difficulty of choosing a companion for Charlie's factory visit. Debate the arguments for and against choosing other family members. Do the children agree that Grandpa Joe deserves to be chosen?

- Direct the children to Mr Wonka's invitation in Chapter 12. Point out the formal language, interesting expressions and abundance of adjectives. What impression does the style give of Mr Wonka's personality?

- Examine the double-spread illustration in Chapter 13. How do the children react to it? Does it make them laugh? Do they feel sorry for Charlie and Grandpa Joe because they look poorer? What do the children think Quentin Blake's intention is?

- Consider the title, focus and setting of Chapter 14. Ask: *Why could this chapter be a story highpoint? Is it important that this is Mr Wonka's first appearance in the book?* Share views.

- Ask the children to do a character study of Mr Wonka, using the information they have by the end of Chapter 14. Enlist ideas from everyone and make a list of characteristics on the whiteboard. The children could progress to using page 31 of *Read and Respond Charlie and the Chocolate Factory.*

- Focus on the language used in Chapter 14 by investigating detailed physical descriptions of Mr Wonka: his eyes, face and jerky movements. Ask the children to identify four words that they think are used effectively.

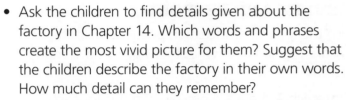

• Ask the children to find details given about the factory in Chapter 14. Which words and phrases create the most vivid picture for them? Suggest that the children describe the factory in their own words. How much detail can they remember?

Ask the children, whenever appropriate, to revisit the text to exemplify/support their answers.

Encourage the children to read aloud back to the group when referring back to the text – praise clear, confident and expressive reading.

## ASSESSMENT OPPORTUNITIES

The following bank of question prompts provides a quick and easy means of monitoring the children's comprehension skills and understanding of the text. The children's answers to a question must be supported by evidence from the text.

### Understanding

• What is strange about the way Mr Wonka shakes hands?

• How many people does Mr Wonka lead on his factory tour?

• How does Mr Wonka show anxiety about the children's visit going wrong?

• Where in the world do Mr Wonka's workers come from?

• Why does the factory have underground rooms?

• Which important door does Mr Wonka stop at finally?

### Inferences

• Why does Charlie comment on the factory's warmth?

• What warnings does Mr Wonka give the party once they are inside the gates?

• Why does Mr Wonka emphasise the need not to dawdle as they walk around?

• Why is the chocolate factory compared to 'a gigantic rabbit warren'?

• What impression does the author want you to have of Mr Wonka by the end of Chapter 14?

### Predicting

• What might happen in Chapter 15?

### Main ideas

• What is interesting about the other four children? Does the author make a clear distinction between Charlie and the other children?

• Is Chapter 14 an important point in the story? Why?

### Language, structure and presentation

• In Chapter 14, why does the author use short sentences and exclamation marks for much of Mr Wonka's speech? Do you think that the style matches the character? How?

• Identify a simile in Chapter 14.

• What is a 'verruca'?

• What is a 'mink coat'? Is it unusual for a young girl to wear one? Why?

# SESSION 5: CHORAL MESSAGES

## SESSION AIMS

Prepare poems to read aloud and perform.

## BEFORE THE SESSION

The children should have read Chapter 16 prior to the session.

## READ

- Ask the children to talk to a partner about what has happened in the story so far and to scan Chapters 15 and 16 independently to remind themselves of recent events.

- Involve the children in a brief group discussion. Ask them:
  - Who eats a big handful of grass?
  - Why does Mrs Salt argue with Mr Wonka about Loompaland?
  - Who starts shouting for an Oompa-Loompa?

- Ask the children: *What words does the author use in Chapter 15 to describe the visitors' reactions to the chocolate river?* (This question focuses on the author's language, its sound and meaning.) Then ask them to read Chapter 17 independently, keeping this question in mind.

### During reading

- Ask the children to think about the information and the questions that arise for them as they read.

- If your school uses reading journals then the children should be encouraged to make notes as they read and consider each question.

- Move around the group and 'tune in' to hear individuals read aloud. Encourage and praise good expression.

## REVISIT AND RESPOND

Use the following discussion points to help the children think about what they have read in more depth.

**Note:** Since there are only 20 minutes for each session, you are advised to focus on only one or two of the elements that are listed below.

- Examine Mr Wonka's feelings about the chocolate room. Ask the children: *Does he enjoy sharing it? What emotions does he show? How are his feelings obvious?* Encourage group discussion. What experience do the children have of displaying something they are proud of?

- Consider the effect that being inside the chocolate room has on the visitors. Ask the children: *Are the visitors impressed by what they see? Are they quieter than usual? Which of Mr Wonka's creations in the chocolate room impresses them the most? Why do you think this?*

- Investigate the sighting of the Oompa-Loompas in Chapter 15. Who first sees them? What is noticeable about them? Do the visitors think that they are likely to be toys, models or real people? Why? What do the children think they would believe if they were one of the visitors?

- Summarise Mr Wonka's recount of how and why the Oompa-Loompas came to the factory. How do the visitors react to his story? Are they interested? Ask the children to put themselves in the visitors' position. Would they believe what they were being told? Why?

- Investigate Augustus Gloop's accident. Let the children bring the story to life in a series of tableaux or freeze-frames.

- Examine Mr Wonka's reaction to Augustus Gloop's accident. Does he find it upsetting or funny? Is he worried or relaxed? Share opinions and ask the children to supply evidence to support their views.

- Direct the children to the song in Chapter 17. Can they identify the message contained in the words? Whose attitude do the children think is reflected in the words? Does this attitude belong to Mr Wonka and the author? Do the children agree with the attitude?

- Suggest that the children do a group performance of the song in Chapter 17. They could divide the song into parts and must think about both the meaning and sound of the lines.

Ask the children, whenever appropriate, to revisit the text to exemplify/support their answers.

Encourage the children to read aloud back to the group when referring back to the text – praise clear, confident and expressive reading.

## ASSESSMENT OPPORTUNITIES

The following bank of question prompts provides a quick and easy means of monitoring the children's comprehension skills and understanding of the text. The children's answers to a question must be supported by evidence from the text.

### Understanding
- Why is Mrs Gloop worried that Augustus will drown in the chocolate river?
- What does Augustus get sucked into?
- Where will the pipe take Augustus?
- Who appears at three clicks of Mr Wonka's fingers?
- What does the Oompa-Loompa do when he looks at Mrs Gloop?
- Where will the Oompa-Loompa find Augustus?
- Why is it important to find Augustus quickly?

### Inferences
- Does Mr Wonka feel worried about Augustus?
- How worried does Mr Gloop seem?
- Why does Mr Wonka say 'your darling boy' when he talks to Mrs Gloop? Does it show affection?

- Why does the Oompa-Loompa start laughing when he looks at Mrs Gloop?
- Why does Mrs Gloop let out a shriek of fury when Mr Wonka says 'my fudge would become quite uneatable'.

### Predicting
- What might happen in Chapter 18? Where will Mr Wonka take the visitors next?

### Main ideas
- Is the factory visit going well? What worrying incident occurs? Is this a sign of things to come?
- Consider Mr Wonka's attitude to Augustus Gloop and his parents. How do Augustus and Mr and Mrs Gloop differ from Charlie and Grandpa Joe? Is the author emphasising that harm will come to a child who is not taught to think of others?

### Language, structure and presentation
- Point out that Chapter 17 contains a new setting. Where are the characters? Why are the settings important to the story? Is there a contrast between some of the settings described so far?
- How does the expression of the Oompa-Loompas differ from that of the other characters? Do the Oompa-Loompas speak in poetry or prose? What do you notice about the rhyme?
- What is a synonym for 'gall'?
- What is a 'louse'?
- What does the expression 'bear a grudge' mean?

### Themes and conventions
- What point is the author making about the effect of letting children be greedy?

# SESSION 6: ACCIDENTS

## SESSION AIMS

Read books that are structured in different ways.

## BEFORE THE SESSION

The children should have read Chapter 20 prior to the session.

## READ

- Ask the children to talk to a partner about what has happened in the story so far and to scan Chapters 19 and 20 independently to remind themselves of recent events.

- Involve the children in a brief group discussion. Ask them:

  - What room has the party reached?

  - What is unusual about allowing the visitors in this room?

  - What is special about the toffee Mr Wonka is making?

- Ask the children: *What do you notice about the title and content of Chapter 19?* (This question focuses on the story's structure.) Then ask them to read Chapter 21 independently, keeping this question in mind.

### During reading

- Ask the children to think about the information and the questions that arise for them as they read.

- If your school uses reading journals then the children should be encouraged to make notes as they read and consider each question.

- Move around the group and 'tune in' to hear individuals read aloud. Encourage and praise good expression.

## REVISIT AND RESPOND

Use the following discussion points to help the children think about what they have read in more depth.

**Note:** Since there are only 20 minutes for each session, you are advised to focus on only one or two of the elements that are listed below.

- Examine Mr Wonka's relationship with the children when he is in the Inventing Room. How does he speak to them? Is he polite? Ask the group to imagine how they would feel if they were in the room with Mr Wonka.

- Investigate the text of Chapter 19. Ask the children to identify examples of warnings given to the children by Mr Wonka. What do the children think this shows about Mr Wonka's state of mind and the children's behaviour?

- Check the length of Chapters 19 and 20. Can the children suggest why the author has made Chapter 20 so short? What reason could he have for not joining it to Chapter 19?

- Direct the children to the titles of Chapters 19, 20 and 21. Do the children find the titles mysterious or interesting? What is the author trying to achieve? Let the children put themselves in the author's place and decide on the titles they would use. Would their titles still fit the structure of this story?

- Consider the language used about the machine in Chapter 20. As the children identify examples of alliteration and onomatopoeia, write them on the whiteboard. Ask the children: *What effect do the words have?*

- Examine the emotions experienced by different characters as Violet chews the chewing-gum meal. Encourage the children to put themselves in Violet's place and express how they feel.

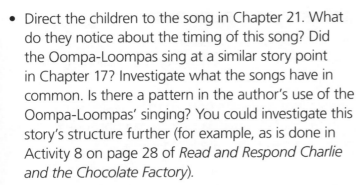

- Direct the children to the song in Chapter 21. What do they notice about the timing of this song? Did the Oompa-Loompas sing at a similar story point in Chapter 17? Investigate what the songs have in common. Is there a pattern in the author's use of the Oompa-Loompas' singing? You could investigate this story's structure further (for example, as is done in Activity 8 on page 28 of *Read and Respond Charlie and the Chocolate Factory*).

Ask the children, whenever appropriate, to revisit the text to exemplify/support their answers.

Encourage the children to read aloud back to the group when referring back to the text – praise clear, confident and expressive reading.

## ASSESSMENT OPPORTUNITIES

The following bank of question prompts provides a quick and easy means of monitoring the children's comprehension skills and understanding of the text. The children's answers to a question must be supported by evidence from the text.

### Understanding

- What is special about Mr Wonka's chewing gum?
- Does Mr Wonka give the gum to Violet?
- What is the first taste that she has?
- Why does Violet's nose turn blue?
- Which part of Mr Wonka's chewing-gum meal always goes wrong for Mr Wonka?
- Which room is Violet taken to by boat?

### Inference

- Why are Mr and Mrs Beauregarde proud when Violet first starts chewing Mr Wonka's gum?
- Why does Charlie watch Violet chew, spellbound?
- Why does Mr Wonka sigh when Violet changes colour?

- Why does Violet stop saying much?
- How do the Oompa-Loompas feel about the swollen, purple Violet?

### Predicting

- What might happen in Chapter 22?

### Main ideas

- How does the author add a serious tone to a story that is often funny? Why could the reader worry about the children in the group of visitors?
- Why does the author let characters be rude to some of the children in the story? Is the author expressing his own views through these characters?

### Language, structure and presentation

- How did the author decide where to end these chapters? Do the chapters end at interesting times? Would you change the structure?
- What is a 'gobstopper'?
- What is a synonym for 'ludicrous'?
- Why is 'disgusted' used to describe Mike Teavee's reaction when he sees Mr Wonka's chewing gum?

# ▼ SESSION 7: BEHAVIOUR

## SESSION AIMS

Identify themes and conventions.

## BEFORE THE SESSION

The children should have read Chapter 24 prior to the session.

## READ

- Ask the children to talk to a partner about what has happened in the story so far and to scan Chapter 24 independently or with a partner, to remind themselves of recent events.
- Involve the children in a brief group discussion. Ask:
  - What does Veruca want?
  - What do Veruca and her parents fall down?
  - Is it surprising that the Oompa-Loompas sing? Why?
- Ask the children: *Why does Veruca demand one of the squirrels?* (This question focuses on the behaviour of children and the attitude of their parents.) Then ask the children to read Chapter 25 independently, keeping this question in mind.

### During reading

- Ask the children to think about the information and the questions that arise for them as they read.
- If your school uses reading journals then the children should be encouraged to make notes as they read and consider each question.
- Move around the group and 'tune in' to hear individuals read aloud. Encourage and praise good expression.

## REVISIT AND RESPOND

Use the following discussion points to help the children think about what they have read in more depth.

**Note:** Since there are only 20 minutes for each session, you are advised to focus on only one or two of the elements that are listed below.

- Investigate the effect of Veruca's demands on her parents in Chapter 24. Do they refuse her request? How does Veruca behave when told not to do something? Ask the children to discuss and list what happens to her and her parents.
- Point out Mr Wonka's comment 'Don't worry' after Veruca disappears down the chute. How does Mr Wonka seem to feel? Encourage the children to share thoughts about what they would feel and say if they were Mr Wonka. Would they be worried when her parents also went down the chute?
- Consider the reaction of the Oompa-Loompas to the Salts' accident. Discuss their song. What is the song's message?
- Point out Mr Wonka's warning against touching 'dangerous stuff'. Do the children think that the author is preparing them for another accident? Encourage discussion as the children consider what and who could be involved.
- Do the children think it is wrong of Mr Wonka to allow the squirrels to push Mr and Mrs Salt down the chute? Why does Mr Wonka let the animals do it? What would the children do if they were in Mr Wonka's situation? Encourage group discussion or you could create a conscience alley for Mr Wonka or the squirrels (see, for example, Activity 5 on page 34 of *Read and Respond Charlie and the Chocolate Factory*).
- Compare Charlie's behaviour with that of the other remaining child, Mike Teavee, during Chapter 25. Ask: *Who is excited about everything? Why is Mike Teavee interested only in television?* Share opinions about what Mr Wonka is thinking and feeling now about each child.

- Point out that lack of control in an important theme in Chapter 25. Ask the children to discuss how Mr Wonka is 'losing' children. Ask them: *Do Charlie and Grandpa feel nervous about what is happening? Does the lift seem safe?* Do the children have experiences of being in situations that are both exciting and scary? Have they, like Charlie and Grandpa Joe, not known what would happen next? Encourage them to share personal experiences.

Ask the children, whenever appropriate, to revisit the text to exemplify/support their answers.

Encourage the children to read aloud back to the group when referring back to the text – praise clear, confident and expressive reading.

## ASSESSMENT OPPORTUNITIES

The following bank of question prompts provides a quick and easy means of monitoring the children's comprehension skills and understanding of the text. The children's answers to a question must be supported by evidence from the text.

### Understanding
- Who complains that his feet are tired?
- How is Mr Wonka's lift different from ordinary lifts?
- Which button does Mike Teavee press?
- Why does Charlie hang on to Grandpa Joe's legs?
- Why is Mr Wonka worried about his hat being spoiled?
- What warning does Mr Wonka give when the lift doors open?

### Inferences
- What does Mr Wonka mean when he says that the disappearing children will 'all come out in the wash'?
- Why does Mr Wonka find the lift ride so funny?
- Why does Grandpa Joe compare the lift ride to being on a roller coaster?
- How dangerous would it be if the two lifts were being used at the same time?
- What does Mr Teavee mean when he says 'Some ride!'?

### Predicting
- What might happen in Chapter 26? Will Mr Wonka carry on losing children?

### Main ideas
- What is the importance of Chapter 25? Is the story reaching an important point? Encourage discussion as the children justify their answers with reference to the text.
- Do the children think that the author is increasing the strangeness of both Mr Wonka and his chocolate factory in Chapter 25? Is Mr Wonka's final speech important?

### Language, structure and presentation
- Point out that Chapter 25 has a change of setting, focus and atmosphere from previous chapters, with the characters inside the 'craziest' lift Charlie has ever seen. Point out Mr Wonka's lack of concern about the speed and possible danger of the ride. Is Dahl emphasising the outrageousness of his character? Does Mr Wonka want his passengers to enjoy the ride? Is he testing the children in some way?
- List details that the author mentions in Chapter 25 to emphasise the movement felt inside the glass lift.
- What are 'jujubes'?
- What is a synonym (an alternative word of the same meaning) for 'tamper'?

### Themes and conventions
- How is lack of control an important theme in Chapter 25?

**SESSION 8:** BREAKING OUT

## SESSION AIMS

Predict what might happen.

## BEFORE THE SESSION

The children should have read Chapter 28 prior to the session.

## READ

- Ask the children to talk to a partner about what has happened in the story so far and to scan Chapter 28 independently to remind themselves of recent events.

- Involve the children in a brief group discussion. Ask them:
  - How does Mr Wonka seem to feel about Charlie being the only child left?
  - What is unusual about the lift?
  - Why does Mr Wonka want the lift to go faster?

- Ask the children: *What seems likely to be the lasting effect for Violet of changing into a blueberry?* (This question focuses on the reader predicting what might happen from details stated and implied.) Then ask them to read Chapters 29 and 30 independently, keeping this type of question in mind.

### During reading

- Ask the children to think about the information and the questions that arise for them as they read.

- If your school uses reading journals then the children should be encouraged to make notes as they read and consider each question.

- Move around the group and 'tune in' to hear individuals read aloud. Encourage and praise good expression.

## REVISIT AND RESPOND

Use the following discussion points to help the children think about what they have read in more depth.

**Note:** Since there are only 20 minutes for each session, you are advised to focus on only one or two of the elements that are listed below.

- Consider the morality of Mr Wonka's actions as he sends four children home in a shocked and changed state. Ask the children: *Should Mr Wonka have taken better care of them? Could he have saved them? Is he being unfeeling when he laughs about them? Should he have invited them into his factory?* Do the children think that that Mr Wonka's behaviour is 'right'? What arguments can they make for and against his behaviour?

- Examine the relationship between Charlie and Mr Wonka in Chapter 28. How does Mr Wonka feel about Charlie being the last remaining child? How does he treat him? Does Charlie show more self-confidence in Chapters 29 and 30? Ask the children to discuss and list the different strengths of the two characters.

- Direct the children to the final three paragraphs of Chapter 28. Ask them to re-read them and to put themselves in the place of Charlie or Grandpa Joe. How do they feel as they hover over the town?

- Hold a group discussion about who is responsible for what has happened to the four children going home in Chapter 29. Is it Mr Wonka, the children's parents or the children themselves? Can the group come to a decision?

- Discuss the events of Chapters 29 and 30. Encourage the children to consider the chapters in relation to the whole book. Are there plot questions from earlier in the book that the author has still not answered? Invite the group to compile a list.

- Question the children about the function of Chapter 30. Ask them: *Does the chapter satisfy the requirements for an ending? Does the chapter finish well? Why?* You could plan a new ending (you could use Activity 6 on page 20 of *Read and Respond Charlie and the Chocolate Factory* to support this work).

- Comment that dialogue is important in this final chapter. Let the children re-read some conversations. What do they reveal about the characters' feelings towards one another?

- Discuss the structure of this book. How is it divided? Do the children think the author could have organised the book in a different way? Share ideas.

- Suggest that an author could decide to write a sequel to this story. Share predictions about what might happen in the new book.

Ask the children, whenever appropriate, to revisit the text to exemplify/support their answers.

Encourage the children to read aloud back to the group when referring back to the text – praise clear, confident and expressive reading.

## ASSESSMENT OPPORTUNITIES

The following bank of question prompts provides a quick and easy means of monitoring the children's comprehension skills and understanding of the text. The children's answers to a question must be supported by evidence from the text.

### Understanding

- What does Charlie tell Mr Wonka that he feels about the factory?

- What does Mr Wonka decide to give Charlie as a present?

- Why did Mr Wonka send out Golden Tickets?

- What does Mr Wonka decide to do about Charlie's family?

- How does the glass lift get into the Buckets' little cottage?

- How do Mr Wonka, Grandpa Joe and Charlie persuade the grandparents to go into the lift?

### Inferences

- Does Mr Wonka feel guilty as he watches the four changed children going home?

- Is it important to Mr Wonka that Charlie says he loves the factory?

- Is Mr Wonka quick to find solutions to problems?

- Does Charlie have more to say now that he has seen inside the chocolate factory?

- What helps the grandparents to feel better about being in the flying lift?

### Main ideas

- Is Charlie happier at the end of the story or at the beginning? Why? Do you think he will keep thinking about this day? Why?

- Consider what has happened to Charlie. Has Mr Wonka made a wise choice? Will Charlie and his family be happy in the chocolate factory?

### Language, structure and presentation

- Examine the illustration in Chapter 30. Does it make an important contribution to the chapter? What does it reveal about the characters shown?

- What does the dialogue in the final chapter reveal about the characters' feelings towards one another?

- What is an 'elevator'? What word is more often used in English?

- Why is 'eat' in *italics* in at the end of Chapter 30? How is Charlie saying the word? What do the italics reveal about his new feelings about life?

# ▼ SESSION 1: MEET VARJAK

## SESSION AIMS

Explore beginnings: introducing characters, settings and plot possibilities.

## BEFORE THE SESSION

The children should have read Chapters 1 to 3 prior to the session.

## READ

- Hold a quick group recall session, to summarise what the children remember. Model recall technique with targeted questions such as:
  - How and where does the story begin?
  - Which characters did you like or dislike?
  - What happened in the first three chapters?

- Remind the children that asking questions (what, why, when, where, who and how) not only helps recall information but can also clarify understanding. Furthermore, reading actively – coming up with their own questions – will help them develop their ideas and make predictions by linking their prior experience of structure, genre and convention to the story as they read.

- Encourage the children to note important parts and link any questions that arise for them during their recall to supporting evidence for discussion; they can do this using sticky notes, marker tabs or a jotter/whiteboard.

## REVISIT AND RESPOND

Use the following discussion points to help the children think about what they have read in more depth.

**Note:** Since there are only 20 minutes for each session, you are advised to focus on only one or two of the elements listed below.

- Ask the children to discuss the characters and categorise whether they are likely to be major or minor characters. Encourage them to note how the author gets them to identify with or dislike the characters, for example through descriptive detail.

- Analyse the introduction of the Gentleman. How does the author imply he is a threat? Why is the illustration of him drawn at a low angle? Is the author's portrayal of him fair, especially considering the gift of the toy mouse and the caviar? Why do the Family appear unworried by the Gentleman, unlike Varjak and the Elder Paw?

- Examine whether Jalal and the Contessa can be considered characters and ask the children to predict whether they will play a meaningful role.

- Focus on the central character, Varjak. What is his relationship like with his family? How is his relationship with the Elder Paw different? Why is Varjak so drawn to stories of Jalal?

- Given Jalal is their revered ancestor, why do the Family seem to scorn tales about Jalal and the respect the Elder Paw has for him? How do the family's reactions make Varjak feel? Ask the children: *How would you feel in his situation?*

- The main characters are cats. How do the cats seem similar or different to humans in a family? What sort of people would you describe them as? How do the Family regard themselves? Why did the author choose cats as the main characters? Ask: *How would the story be different if Varjak were a boy or girl of your age at a local school?*

- Encourage the children to examine the initial setting for the book. What do they know about the Contessa's house? What is a Contessa? Ask them to consider whether the story is modern, historical or timeless. Why might the author have made this choice?

- Examine the main ideas related to the plot. What do the children think has happened? What does the Elder Paw think has happened and what does he think they should do? What happens at the Family Council?

- Encourage a focus on language and descriptive detail, especially verbs. How do they suggest character, mood and intention?

- Discuss the impact of the illustrations. How would the children describe their style? Would it be the same listening to the book rather than reading it? How does the illustrator use illustrations to shape our opinion of character?

- Analyse the characteristics of an engaging beginning. How does the author engage the reader's interest? Who is telling the story? How can you tell?

Ask the children, whenever appropriate, to revisit the text to exemplify/support their answers.

Encourage the children to read aloud back to the group when referring back to the text – praise clear, confident and expressive reading.

## ASSESSMENT OPPORTUNITIES

The following bank of question prompts provides a quick and easy means of monitoring the children's comprehension skills and understanding of the text. The children's answers to a question must be supported by evidence from the text.

### Understanding

- Why does Varjak like tales about his ancestor Jalal?
- What words and phrases tell you how Varjak feels about life in the Contessa's house?
- What shows that the power in the Family has changed by the end of Chapter 3?
- Why have things changed for the Family?
- What questions would you ask the Paws about their life?

### Inferences

- Is Julius right about why the cats never see the Contessa?
- Compare and contrast how Varjak and the Family react to the Gentleman's gift of a toy mouse. Why do you think they react so differently?
- The saying 'Never judge a book by its cover' suggests character is not related to looks. Do you think this is true in the book? Give examples from the text.

### Predicting

- Is Father or the Elder Paw right about the Gentleman?
- What do you think Varjak will do after the Family Council?
- How might the expression 'Pride comes before a fall' be relevant to the Family?
- How do these chapters set up the plot?
- What do you predict will be the central problem or conflict in the story?

### Main ideas

- Summarise the significant events in the first three chapters.
- Why is the Family fearful of Outside? Do they have good reasons?
- How is Varjak different to his family and how does it set him up as the central character?

### Language, structure and presentation

- How do the illustrations add impact to the story?
- Why is Outside written with a capital letter?
- What other text effects does the author use?

### Themes and conventions

- Home is meant to be a secure place for children. What does 'home' seem like for Varjak?
- What is the benefit of using cats as the central characters?
- Why did the author choose a timeless setting that is hard to place?

# ▼ SESSION 2: VENTURING OUTSIDE

## SESSION AIMS

Identify, describe and compare different settings in the story.

## BEFORE THE SESSION

The children should have read up to Chapter 9 prior to the session.

## READ

- Ask the children to recall the different places mentioned so far in the story. Ask: *Where does the story begin? Where does Varjak go to in his dreams? What does he see over the wall?*

- Skim Chapter 8, noting how Varjak's environment changes when he leaves the house. While skimming, ask the children to:
  - consider how different it is Outside
  - identify the new sights, sounds and smells Varjak experiences
  - imagine how differently each place made Varjak feel.

- Outside, Varjak faces things he never had to worry about before – what are they?

- Read Chapter 9 together with the children, keeping the following questions in mind: *Why did Varjak enter the hut? What is it like in there? Who else is in the hut? Does he feel welcome?*

## REVISIT AND RESPOND

Use the following discussion points to help the children think about what they have read in more depth.

**Note:** Since there are only 20 minutes for each session, you are advised to focus on only one or two of the elements that are listed below.

- Compare and contrast the setting and atmosphere of Chapter 8 with that of Chapter 9. Identify similarities and differences.

- Then compare and contrast the description of the house in Chapter 1 with that of the hut at the end of Chapter 8 and in Chapter 9, and identify similarities and differences.

- What evidence is there that Varjak feels safe or unsafe in the hut?

- Describe the various emotions Varjak experiences from entering the hut to falling asleep. Which emotions can the children relate too?

- Have any children in the group had to leave home or move cities? How did they feel? Was it easy or difficult to adjust to a new place and make friends?

- Focus on the descriptions of the weather, the time of day, the light and the temperature inside and outside the hut. How do they add to the general atmosphere? How do they reflect how Varjak is feeling?

- The first few chapters make it difficult to place the setting. What additional information is given in Chapters 8 and 9 to tell the reader where or when this story takes place?

- Given how Varjak has handled the situation so far, ask the children to predict how he will adapt to being Outside. What is his driving force?

Ask the children, whenever appropriate, to revisit the text to exemplify/support their answers.

Encourage the children to read aloud back to the group when referring back to the text – praise clear, confident and expressive reading.

## ASSESSMENT OPPORTUNITIES

The following bank of question prompts provides a quick and easy means of monitoring the children's comprehension skills and understanding of the text. The children's answers to a question must be supported by evidence from the text.

### Understanding

- Who is the other cat in the hut and how is she different from Varjak?

- Why was the hut a suitable 'shelter' for Varjak? What was it sheltering the cats from? What other purpose could the hut have?

- Describe how Varjak feels inside the hut – physically and emotionally.
- Who made the 'invisible barrier' between them? What does it tell you about the other cat?
- What do the two cats talk about? Who asks most of the questions? Why did Varjak feel he could not say everything he was thinking?
- What has Varjak experienced and learned about the Outside from Holly? How does he feel about being Outside?
- On what condition does the other cat agree to let Varjak stay for the night?

## Inferences

- From the other cat's introduction, what can you tell about her?
- What words tell us that Varjak wasn't scared of the other cat?
- How did the other cat react when Varjak told her he was 'special'? According to her, what makes someone special?
- Why did the other cat relax when she saw that Varjak was wearing a collar?
- The other cat doesn't use Varjak's name, instead she calls him 'Special Cat' and 'pet cat'. What do these names imply?
- Explain the significance of the cats wearing or not wearing a collar.

## Predicting

- What do you think Varjak might encounter when he leaves the hut?
- Will Varjak and the other cat become friends? How can you tell?
- Varjak expresses many unanswered questions about the Outside. What are these questions and do you think he will find the answers?
- In what way is this chapter (and the scene in the hut) part of the plot?

## Main ideas

- Compare the hut to the Contessa's house. Summarise the similarities and the differences.
- How has Varjak's situation changed since he left the house? Compare his life then to how it is now and summarise the similarities and differences.
- Where does Varjak want to be? Explain why.

## Language, structure and presentation

- Identify the simile in the first sentence. What does it tell you about the hut?
- Explain the expression: 'You're so high and mighty.' Who used this expression and was it used as a compliment, an insult or a general statement?
- List the adjectives used to describe a) the hut and b) the weather in Chapter 9.
- How would you describe the tone of the conversation between the two cats? What words suggest this?
- What does the exclamation mark in 'It was another cat!' indicate? What does it tell you about how Varjak was feeling?
- What questions do you have about the scene in the hut? Are you interested to know the cat's name or if there are other cats staying there?

## Themes and conventions

- Look at the picture of the hut on the first page of Chapter 9. What impact does it have on the reader? What does it reveal about Varjak's situation?
- What does Varjak learn about himself and his feelings towards home in this chapter? What themes does this reflect?
- The hut is the place where these two characters meet for the first time. What do they learn about each other?
- Explain how this chapter sets the scene for the rest of the plot to unfold. (Consider the questions that Varjak asks himself and their role in the story.)

# ▼ SESSION 3: FIRST ENCOUNTERS

## SESSION AIMS

Consider the author's use of language, including figurative language, the impact on the reader and how it contributes to meaning.

## BEFORE THE SESSION

The children should have read Chapters 10 and 11 independently prior to the session.

## READ

- Ask the children to recall the events in Chapters 10 and 11 using these questions to prompt their memory:
  - What skill did Varjak learn in the second dream?
  - Why does he need this skill now? What does he need to do?
  - Whom does he meet for the first time in Chapter 11?
  - How do the other cats react to him?
  - Why does Varjak end up alone at the end of Chapter 11?
- Now ask the children to skim Chapter 12, looking only at the pictures. As they view the pictures, they should try to predict what will happen next. Ask them:
  - What does Varjak encounter in the street?
  - As this object gets closer to Varjak, what does it start to resemble?
- The first four pictures show the reader what Varjak saw from his perspective. From the pictures, how do you think he was feeling?
- The final picture shows what happened from the perspective of an onlooker (or the reader.) Ask the children to explain what they can see.
- Read Chapter 12 with the children. Encourage them to focus on how the text and the pictures support each other. They should check to see if their predictions were correct.

## REVISIT AND RESPOND

Use the following discussion points to help the children think about what they have read in more depth.

**Note:** Since there are only 20 minutes for each session, you are advised to focus on only one or two of the elements that are listed below.

- How does the author use the description of the sky and the weather to reflect Varjak's feelings of loneliness?
- When Varjak sees the streetlights he thinks they are trees, yet they are different to the trees in his dream and the ones at the Contessa's house. Why did he mistake them for trees? Compare and contrast their similarities and differences.
- The author describes things in the city from Varjak's perspective. What does this mean? Find examples of this in Chapters 11 and 12 and explain the effect this has on the reader.
- Varjak is constantly learning things about his 'new' environment. What further information about Outside does he discover in this chapter?
- Identify the climax of the chapter. How does the author manipulate the text to give impact to the climax? Consider the use of capitals, dashes, short lines and spacing.
- Did Varjak successfully apply the second skill of the Way in Chapter 12: 'assume nothing; be sure of the facts'? What did he assume? What facts was he relying on? What could he have done to avoid the mistake?
- At the end of the chapter, Varjak believes he has failed. Ask the children: *What exactly did he fail at? If you could speak to Varjak, what advice or encouragement would you give him at this point?*
- Ask the children to imagine being part of the group of people who witnessed this incident. How would they have reacted as a bystander?
- When Varjak stepped out in the road to face the 'dogs' he was being selfless and brave at the same time. What does it mean to be selfless?

Ask the children, whenever appropriate, to revisit the text to exemplify/support their answers.

Encourage the children to read aloud back to the group when referring back to the text – praise clear, confident and expressive reading.

## ASSESSMENT OPPORTUNITIES

The following bank of question prompts provides a quick and easy means of monitoring the children's comprehension skills and understanding of the text. The children's answers to a question must be supported by evidence from the text.

### Understanding
- Despite how he felt at the beginning of the chapter, Varjak was focused on his mission. What three things was he determined to achieve? (Notice the author's use of the rule of three.)
- Why did Varjak not want to be seen by the group of people?
- When Varjak saw and touched the parked cars, what did he assume?
- List the emotions Varjak experiences throughout Chapter 12.
- At the end of the chapter, Varjak believes he has failed. Why does he think this?

### Inferences
- Why did Varjak feel exposed in the glare of the streetlamps?
- Why did Varjak's fur prickle when he saw a group of people?
- How do we know that Varjak was scared?
- When Varjak faced the oncoming 'beast', why did he remember the Elder Paw in the garden?
- What do you think about Varjak's plan of action? Considering what he knew about the city and the 'dogs', was it a good plan?

### Predicting
- Varjak is shocked by his near-death experience. What questions do you think he might ask himself after these events?

- How do you think Varjak feels? Will he recover from having 'failed'?

### Main ideas
- Why did Varjak think the cars were dogs? List all the things that made him believe this.
- How did Varjak feel before and after his encounter?
- Summarise Chapters 10, 11 and 12 using one sentence for each.

### Language, structure and presentation
- Explain the terms 'being alone' and 'feeling lonely'.
- The author uses comparisons to describe things. Identify the comparisons in this chapter and decide if they are similes or metaphors.
- Is the expression 'he froze in his tracks' literal or figurative? Explain what this expression means and how Varjak felt and behaved.
- Notice how the author uses short sentences and single-word exclamations to quicken the pace and create tension in the text. Identify examples of this, especially in the build up to the climax and at the end of the chapter.

### Themes and conventions
- Varjak understood his mission, but he failed at his first attempt. Is giving up an option for him? What do you think he must learn to do now, and what theme does this reflect?
- Throughout the story there are characters we never meet. Why do you think the author does not mention the drivers of the cars, for example? What effect does this have on the reader?
- Facing the 'dogs' was not easy for Varjak: he was torn between doing something he didn't want to do and something he felt he had to do. Identify parts of the text that showed how he wrestled with himself.

# SESSION 4: DREAMING

## SESSION AIMS

Look at structure, presentation and writing conventions. Focus on character development.

## BEFORE THE SESSION

The children should have read Chapters 13 to 15 prior to the session.

## READ

- Ask the children to briefly summarise to each other what happened in Chapters 13 to 15 by discussing what happened immediately before Chapter 13 and the main point of each chapter.

- Get the children to re-read the chapters with these focus questions in mind:
  - How does Varjak change over the three chapters?
  - How do language and presentation enhance the storytelling?
  - How is the dream chapter linked to the chapters before and after?

- Share the focus questions so pairs read with one aspect in mind.

- Remind the children to use sticky notes, marker tabs or a whiteboard/jotter to keep track of relevant evidence in the text to support their ideas.

- If time is available, allow pairs to give the group feedback on the key points relating to their focus area prior to discussion. Wander around during this time and listen in to the children's overviews.

## REVISIT AND RESPOND

Use the following discussion points to help the children think about what they have read in more depth.

**Note:** Since there are only 20 minutes for each session, you are advised to focus on only one or two of the elements listed below.

- Ask the children: *What is Varjak's mood at the start of Chapter 13? Why is he feeling this way? What is it that Varjak doesn't understand? How do we know Varjak is mistaken in his mission when the word 'car' does not appear?*

- Ask: *Why does Varjak think he can't go home? What does 'can't' mean in this context: something he's physically unable to do or something he doesn't want to do? Do you think his feelings are justified?*

- On the second page of Chapter 13, two short paragraphs are enclosed by the full-page illustration. Ask the children: *How does this layout match the content and emphasise Varjak's mood?* Choose a verb that shows his body language and discuss the effect of 'away' being repeated three times in one paragraph. Find examples of how the surroundings mirror Varjak's feelings.

- Ask the children why Varjak enters the enclosed and desolate courtyard. What does 'he'd lost the moon and stars' mean? Ask: *How would you describe the atmosphere in the alleyway? What might people inside be trying to keep out? What do we do when it gets dark in our homes?*

- Examine how the author builds tension as Varjak creeps into the courtyard. Have the children ever felt their way in dark or unfamiliar surroundings? What is it like?

- Ask the children: *What is the significance of none of the tomcats wearing a collar? Which verbs and phrases contrast the attack to just moments before? How does the placing of the illustration emphasise the fear and violence of the attack? What text effect adds further emphasis?*

- The moments after the attack could be described as Varjak's lowest moment in the story. What evidence supports this? Ask the children: *Do you think things could get worse? How?*

- Ask the children why they think the author presents the dream chapters differently to the main story chapters. What is the significance of the lack of page numbers? Why do they think the illustrations

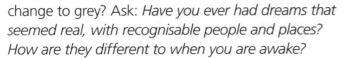

change to grey? Ask: *Have you ever had dreams that seemed real, with recognisable people and places? How are they different to when you are awake?*

- Examine the evocative descriptions in Chapter 14. Identify words and phrases that reveal the pain Varjak feels, that describe the alleyway and that depict the surrounding sounds and smells.

- Compare how Varjak feels physically to how he feels 'inside' when he wakes. Why has his mood lifted?

- Ask: *How is the city divided up among the gangs? Can you think of other stories about belonging to or being part of a gang or particular group of people?*

- Ask: *Why is Varjak doubtful of Tam describing Sally Bones as 'not one of us'? How is Varjak familiar with this feeling? Do you think he feels at home with Jalal? Does he feel at home with Holly and Tam?*

- All the cats fear Sally Bones. Discuss why Sally is so frightening. Are the reasons sound – or could it just be prejudice or jealousy?

- Get the children to compare the three characters – what do their conversations reveal about them? Ask: *Why did Holly save Varjak? Why is Varjak grateful when he felt so miserable before?*

Ask the children, whenever appropriate, to revisit the text to exemplify/support their answers.

Encourage the children to read aloud back to the group when referring back to the text – praise clear, confident and expressive reading.

## ASSESSMENT OPPORTUNITIES

The following bank of question prompts provides a quick and easy means of monitoring the children's comprehension skills and understanding of the text. The children's answers to a question must be supported by evidence from the text.

### Understanding
- Why does Jalal say the cats by the fire may as well be dead?
- How does the skill Jalal teaches respond to Varjak's circumstances?
- In what ways do Holly and Tam agree about Sally Bones?

- Holly is sceptical about Varjak being able to hunt. Is that fair?
- Is Holly being unkind when she teases Tam? What does this show?

### Inferences
- Do you agree with Varjak's self-assessment after his encounter with the 'monsters'?
- What made the tomcats attack Varjak?
- Why did Varjak follow Holly 'without a second thought'?
- What evidence is there of Tam 'always being so dramatic'?
- Why did Varjak say he could hunt? Is hunting a learned skill or just instinct for cats?
- Choose your own words to describe Varjak's mood by the end of your reading.

### Predicting
- Would Jalal think Varjak's family were 'true cats'? Explain your thinking.
- Predict what will happen in the next chapter when the three friends go to the park.

### Language, structure and presentation
- What writer technique allows the reader to understand how the city works?
- What is the purpose in the story of Varjak's regular dreams of Jalal and Mesopotamia?
- What is a 'white wedge of moon'? How does the night sky symbolise that things are looking up for Varjak?

### Themes and conventions
- Where do you think Varjak's home really is? Use evidence from all three chapters in your answer.

# SESSION 5: TIME PASSING

## SESSION AIMS

Consider main ideas and identify key details that support the main ideas through questioning and distinguish between facts and opinion.

## BEFORE THE SESSION

The children should have read Chapters 17 to 21 independently prior to the session.

## READ

- Recall some main events up to Chapter 21 by asking the following questions (the children can skim through previous chapters to find the answers):
  - What skill does Varjak learn about in Chapter 17? Why does he need it?
  - Name Varjak's friends and enemies.
  - After Varjak saves Holly from the pigeons, she says 'I guess we're even now.' What does she mean?
  - How has Varjak changed since he arrived in the city?
  - Why did Tam leave them?
  - Why did Razor attack Varjak? How did Varjak react? Do you think they will meet up again?
- Read Chapter 21 together. While reading, the children should consider the following questions:
  - Where did Holly and Varjak search for Tam? Were they successful?
  - What clues tell the reader that Tam is in danger?
  - What do Holly and Varjak think has happened to Tam?
  - What do you think has happened to Tam?
- The children can make notes as they read.

## REVISIT AND RESPOND

Use the following discussion points to help the children think about what they have read in more depth.

**Note:** Since there are only 20 minutes for each session, you are advised to focus on only one or two of the elements listed below.

- Encourage the children to find clues in Chapter 21 that indicate how much time has elapsed. Consider the references to the moon, Varjak's wounds and his fading memories.
- Read the opening sentence of Chapter 22. Explore the idea of external and internal wounds. How has Varjak suffered both? What might be helping them to heal?
- There is frequent reference to the moon, the stars and the sky. Ask: *Why do you think it is an ever-present part of Varjak's journey? What effect does it have on him? What effect does it have on the reader?*
- Ask the children to identify things that show Holly and Varjak have grown close. What is Varjak surprised to learn about Holly?
- When Varjak sees the animals in the toyshop, what is his reaction? Ask the children to recall other times in the story when Varjak has seen a toy animal.
- Consider what the toy cat says and how it speaks. Ask: *What is a 'tinny' voice? How would you describe the toy cat's statement 'I be your friend forever!' In what way does the toy cat resemble a real cat?* This is not the first time that Varjak is confused; encourage the children to think of other times when Varjak was mistaken.
- Holly and Varjak stop looking for Tam, concluding that she has 'Vanished'. Debate this decision: was it a good or a bad one? Why? The children can work together to think of reasons, then report back.
- Holly tells Varjak that 'people like toy cats better than real cats'. Ask the children: *Is this fact or opinion? Why does Holly think this? What are the*

advantages and disadvantages of having a toy animal rather than a real one? Which one would you prefer? Why?

- Explore why Varjak feels homesick. Can the children empathise with feeling this way? If they have felt this way, how did they handle it? Did someone else help them to feel better? Holly tried to make Varjak feel better. Ask: *What advice did she give? Did it help him to feel better? What advice would you have given him?*

- Compare and contrast Varjak's previous home to where he is now. Why does Varjak feel he doesn't have a home anymore? Let the children discuss their ideas of what 'home' and 'being homeless' mean.

Ask the children, whenever appropriate, to revisit the text to exemplify/support their answers.

Encourage the children to read aloud back to the group when referring back to the text – praise clear, confident and expressive reading.

## ASSESSMENT OPPORTUNITIES

The following bank of question prompts provides a quick and easy means of monitoring the children's comprehension skills and understanding of the text. The children's answers to questions must be supported by evidence from the text.

### Understanding

- Why did Holly decide to stop looking for Tam?
- Varjak said he wanted to go home, but he couldn't. Why?
- What did Holly mean when she said, 'The whole world's your home now'?

### Inferences

- Both Holly and Varjak admit they had a 'bad feeling' about the alleyway where Tam disappeared. What did they mean by this?
- When Varjak insists that the toy cat is Tam, Holly 'snaps' at him. Why did she react in this way? Was she angry with Varjak?

- Holly describes Tam as 'a greedy idiot'. Did she mean it? Why did she say it?
- When Varjak remembers the Contessa's house, why do his memory pictures 'keep changing'?
- At the end of the chapter, we learn that the invisible barrier between Holly and Varjak has gone. What does this tell you about their relationship?

### Predicting

- Holly tells Varjak 'you never know what's around the corner'. What do you think might happen next?
- Based on the references to toys, do you think there might be a link later in the story? Why?

### Main ideas

- How would you group these five chapters into three main ideas?
- What role do the toys play in the story?
- Does this chapter represent a high point or a low point for Varjak on his mission? Explain your thinking.

### Language, structure and presentation

- In Chapter 17, Jalal teaches Varjak the skill of 'Slow-Time'. Identify parts of the text that use a dash to create the effect of slowing down.
- Look at the first picture of the pigeon in Chapter 18. Based on the size of the picture, what does it represent to Varjak?

### Themes and conventions

- Based on the events in Chapter 21, explain the meaning of the theme 'What is real?'.
- Varjak's view of the city from a distance changes when he enters the city. Why does the author describe the trees and buildings as getting bigger?
- Why is the name 'Razor' appropriate? What other names in the book have significance?
- Describe the weather in Chapter 21 and explain how it reflects how Holly and Varjak are feeling.

# ▼ SESSION 6: TURNING POINT

## SESSION AIMS

Predict what might happen from details stated and implied, drawing inferences and asking questions to improve their understanding.

## BEFORE THE SESSION

The children should have read Chapters 22 to 25 independently prior to the session.

## READ

- Encourage the children to recall events in Chapters 22 to 25 by asking the following questions:
  - Varjak has two more dreams. Which new skills does he acquire?
  - Which two main characters are introduced at this point?
  - At the end of Chapter 24, what appears to have happened to Varjak?
  - How do you think Varjak will get out of this situation? What skill do you think he'll use?
- 'Things are not always what they seem'. With this expression in mind, ask the children to turn to Chapter 26 and read it together. Then ask:
  - Did things turn out as you expected?
  - Did Varjak need to use any skills of the Way to save himself?
  - What major realisation does Varjak have in this chapter?

## REVISIT AND RESPOND

Use the following discussion points to help the children think about what they have read in more depth.

**Note:** Since there are only 20 minutes for each session, you are advised to focus on only one or two of the elements listed below.

- Ask the children to look at how the 'monster' appeared to Varjak in Chapters 24 and 26. Why did he not realise it was a dog?
- Consider the placing and timing of the dreams in the story. Ask the children: *At what point in the story do they occur? In what way is the dream in Chapter 25 premature? How can you tell Vajrak will need it in the future?*
- According to Varjak, Cludge is about to eat him. Ask the children to identify the turning point in the chapter. How does the author create this element of surprise? Did anyone predict this would happen? Do the children feel surprised, relieved, irritated or disappointed in the outcome of this event? Why?
- Ask the children to practise talking like Cludge. Ask: *How does he sound? What can you tell about him from the way he speaks? Why does the expression, 'His bark is worse than his bite' fit here?* Can the children find a sentence in the text that expresses this in a slightly different way?
- In the sixth dream, Jalal explains that you can only learn to let go when you know who you are. What does Varjak learn about himself in Chapter 26? In what way does Cludge remind him of himself? How does Varjak feel about himself at the end the chapter? Compare this to the beginning
- When Varjak woke up to face the 'monster' was gone. Ask: *Why did she leave? How m Varjak have felt? Where do you think she went? How do you know she wasn't very far away? Was Varjak upset with her? How would you have reacted if you were Holly? Have you ever felt deserted?*

- Re-read the part where Holly starts to giggle then laugh uncontrollably. Ask: *What does Holly find so funny? Why do the others join in? Are they laughing at Varjak or with him? Explain. What role does this laughter play in the story?* Can the children share a time when they laughed in this way? How did it make them feel? Explain the expression 'laughter is the best medicine.'

- By the end of the chapter, the three characters are friends and teammates. Ask: *What has brought them together? Why are they prepared to help Varjak? How has he earned their respect? What are Holly's and Cludge's reasons for leaving with Varjak? How does Varjak feel now?* Explain the expression 'strength in numbers'.

Ask the children, whenever appropriate, to revisit the text to exemplify/support their answers.

Encourage the children to read aloud back to the group when referring back to the text – praise clear, confident and expressive reading.

## ASSESSMENT OPPORTUNITIES

The following bank of question prompts provides a quick and easy means of monitoring the children's comprehension skills and understanding of the text. The children's answers to a question must be supported by evidence from the text.

### Understanding

- In the dream in Chapter 23, Jalal tells Varjak 'you have travelled far since first we met'. Is he speaking figuratively or literally? What does he mean?

- At the beginning of Chapter 26, why does Varjak doubt himself and think he was wrong to trust his instincts? How had he acted on his instincts?

- What is a 'beginner's mistake' and how does it apply to Varjak?

- Many questions about the story have been answered by the end of Chapter 26. What questions are still to be answered?

### Inferences

- What does Sally realise about Varjak? What do her words 'You? Is it you?' imply?

- Why does Varjak not always succeed in using the skills of the Way successfully? What is the author trying to achieve?

- Compare the way the author describes the cats to the way he describes Cludge. What effect does this have on the reader?

### Predicting

- At the end of Chapter 22, Jalal warns Varjak to 'only cause harm when your life is in danger'. In what way is this warning a prediction of what is to come?

- Sally Bones tells Varjak, 'We'll finish this another time'. Do you think they will meet again?

### Main ideas

- Explain which chapter is the turning point or pivotal moment in the story.

- Consider how Varjak and Holly's relationship has changed. Which character seemed to be in charge at the beginning and how has this changed?

### Language, structure and presentation

- Identify and explain the figurative language in the first paragraph of Chapter 26.

- How does the author use punctuation to express how Cludge speaks? What effect does this create?

- What does the word 'contagious' mean? How does it apply to laughter?

### Themes and conventions

- Identify a picture in Chapter 23 and 24 that summarises each chapter. How do the pictures support the mood of the moment?

- Compare and contrast the tone at the start of Chapter 26 to the tone at the end. Describe how the tone changes.

# SESSION 7: COMING HOME

## SESSION AIMS

Discuss plot structure: stages in a hero's journey/resolution and conclusions.
Make inferences and identify evidence.

## BEFORE THE SESSION

The children should have read chapters 27 to 31 independently prior to the session.

## READ

- Ask the children to remind themselves what happened in Chapters 27 to 31 using these questions:
  - What happens when Varjak gets home?
  - Why did Varjak and Julius fight?
  - What happens to Holly?
  - What final skill does Varjak learn and what does he discover about himself?
- Ask the children to briefly discuss the following points, giving reasons from the text for their views:
  - Has Varjak acted like a true Mesopotamian Blue since returning home?
  - What will happen when he wakes up from his dream?
- Ask the children to read Chapter 32 together, focusing on how and why Varjak's behaviour changes.
- Remind the children to use sticky notes, marker tabs or a whiteboard/jotter to keep track of relevant evidence in the text.

## REVISIT AND RESPOND

Use the following discussion points to help the children think about what they have read in more depth.

**Note:** Since there are only 20 minutes for each session, you are advised to focus on only one or two of the elements that are listed below.

- Ask the children how the weather reflects the storyline as Varjak returns home. Ask: *What does it mean when the moon is described as 'a sullen one-eyed sentry in the sky'? At what other times in the story has the weather or time of day reflected Varjak's situation or mood?*
- When they reach the wall, Varjak thinks everything may have changed since he left. Why is this? Have things changed from the outside? Explore the children's experiences of returning somewhere and finding it no longer as they remember. Ask them: *Had the place changed or had you changed?*
- Ask the children why Varjak didn't tell his family about his dreams. Ask: *How did Varjak's family react to his recount of events? Why do you think Julius is so aggressive towards Varjak? What words show his mood?*
- Varjak's victory tasted 'sweet like cinnamon'. Ask the children: *What sort of figurative language is this? Where else does cinnamon appear in the story and what does it imply about Varjak's victory?*
- Ask the children to look at how Varjak's family greet and treat Holly. Why do they behave like this? Father says that 'common cats are nothing'. Ask: *Can one group of people be more special than another just because of the family they were born into? Is this right?*
- Ask the children what Holly goes off to do without Varjak and his family. Why doesn't Varjak go with her? What was Varjak's mission in the first place? Has he achieved this?
- Ask the children to explain what Holly found upstairs. Can they recall when else Varjak encountered the 'not quite dead not quite alive' sensation?

- Ask the children: *Have you ever been in a situation when the right thing to do is not the easy thing to do? Can you think of any other books where the main character has difficult choices to make? What choices were they? Did the character always make the right choice at first? What influenced the character's decisions?*

- Ask the children what Jasmine's voice sounds like when Varjak first returns. How does it sound by the end of Chapter 30? What does this imply about whether Varjak has really done the right thing, as his mother says?

- What is the seventh skill and why can't Jalal teach it to Varjak? How is it different from the first skill? Which skill do the children think is the most important?

- Ask the children to find a phrase in the text that sums up the Way of Jalal. How does this phrase contrast with what Varjak was taught to believe? Ask the children what they think being 'noble' means.

- Ask: *What does Varjak decide to do when he awakes from his dream? Were you surprised when Varjak's family didn't help him?* The children should give reasons for their answers based on their reading.

- Ask the children what sensation makes Varjak notice the cats in the box. What does he mean by them being 'like the toys in the city – but turned off'? Ask the children to put this into their own words.

- In the final climax of the book, Varjak faces two tests back at the Contessa's house. What are they? Which was the most difficult for Varjak? Ask the children which they thought took more courage.

Ask the children, whenever appropriate, to revisit the text to exemplify/support their answers.

Encourage the children to read aloud back to the group when referring back to the text – praise clear, confident and expressive reading.

## ASSESSMENT OPPORTUNITIES

The following bank of question prompts provides a quick and easy means of monitoring the children's comprehension skills and understanding of the text. The children's answers to a question must be supported by evidence from the text.

### Understanding

- Why couldn't Cludge go with the others into the house?

- Why did Jalal make Varjak look into the river? What did he see? Why was this important to Varjak?

- How did the cats' fear affect Varjak? Can you 'taste' fear? Give an example.

### Inferences

- Father says 'We are different. We are special. We are Mesopotamian Blues.' What makes him say this? How is this attitude similar to that of gangs?

- Why is Varjak sickened by what the tortoiseshell cat says when the Gentleman brings it back?

### Predicting

- How do you think Varjak will resolve the final problem of the cats in the cage?

### Main ideas

- How would you explain to Holly what you think is going on upstairs?

- How do Varjak's actions show he's understood the Seventh Skill?

### Language, structure and presentation

- When Varjak faces Julius, his mind is described as 'catching fire'. What does this mean?

- What words tell you that the toy cats in the box were once real-life cats?

### Themes and conventions

- Varjak thinks he's a true Mesopotamian Blue after he beats Julius. Do you agree?

- Varjak faced a terrible choice at the end of Chapter 30. What did he choose? What would you have chosen? What themes does this link to?

## SESSION AIMS

Identify and discuss themes and character development.
Check the book makes sense to the children, discussing their understanding.

## BEFORE THE SESSION

The children should have read Chapters 33 and 34 independently before the session.

## READ

- Allow time for the children to recap on the momentous events of Chapters 33 and 34. Guide their recap by asking them to consider these questions:
  - What would have happened to the caged cats had Varjak not saved them? How do you know?
  - How did Varjak use what he has learned to succeed in his final challenges?
  - Why were the black cats so hard to beat?
  - How was the Gentleman overcome?
- Ask the children to discuss the following question: *What do Varjak's actions show you about his character and how he has changed from the start of the book?* They should use evidence from the text to support their views.
- Ask the children to read Chapter 35 together, focusing on how the final chapter ties up loose ends and leads into a possible sequel.
- Remind the children that they can make notes or use tabs to mark evidence, to back up their ideas.

## REVISIT AND RESPOND

Use the following discussion points to help the children think about what they have read in more depth.

**Note:** Since there are only 20 minutes for each session, you are advised to focus on only one or two of the elements that are listed below.

- Ask the children: *What happens when Varjak lets the cats out of the cage? What is the problem? What words in the text describe the chaos?*
- When Varjak faces the black cats, he feels calm – as though he had been waiting for this moment all his life. Ask: *What does Varjak mean? How is this different to Varjak's reaction when the black cats attacked the Elder Paw? Why do you think Varjak feels so different now?*
- Discuss the reality theme that runs throughout the book. Were the black cats machines or were they real? Was the danger to Varjak and the other cats real? Is real the same as alive? What evidence suggests the black cats were neither alive nor in fact quite dead?
- Examine other aspects of the reality theme. What is a real family? Was Varjak's family a real family? Who in the book was more like Varjak's family than his actual family?
- Consider *The Wizard of Oz* quotation from the beginning of the book. Ask the children: *Where is Varjak's home? Is it the Contessa's house with his family? Is it in Mesopotamia with Jalal in his dreams? Is it Outside with Holly, Cludge and Tam?*
- Examine what 'home' means to the children. Is it where they live? Have any of them moved house? If they have, has their home changed? Ask: *Can school be seen as home? Can places you often go and stay on holiday or with relatives be seen as home? Can you have more than one home?* Ask the children whether they know other books about finding a new home (for example, *The Secret Garden* by Frances Hodgson Burnett and *The Lion, The Witch and the Wardrobe* by C.S. Lewis).

- Ask: *Why and how did Cludge save the day? How was he able to climb the wall? What does this tell you about friendship and loyalty?*

- Why did Varjak's family choose not to go Outside with him? Was it a good decision for them? For Varjak? Encourage the children to give reasons for their answers.

- Analyse the word 'gang'. Ask: *Where does this word first appear in the book? Why didn't Holly want to be in the gang? Why does Holly now want to be in a gang? From your experience, are gangs good or bad things? Why?*

- Ask the children what Varjak's dreams taught him.

- By the final chapters, how has Varjak changed from when he set out on his quest? Ask the children to consider Varjak's feelings about himself, how his family regard him and how his friends think of him.

- What evidence can the children find in the final chapter to suggest this book may have a sequel? Ask them to consider which characters they think would appear in the next book. Ask: *What would a sequel be about? Would you like to read another book in this series? Why?*

Ask the children, whenever appropriate, to revisit the text to exemplify/support their answers.

Encourage the children to read aloud back to the group when referring back to the text – praise clear, confident and expressive reading.

## ASSESSMENT OPPORTUNITIES

The following bank of question prompts provides a quick and easy means of monitoring the children's comprehension skills and understanding of the text. The children's answers to a question must be supported by evidence from the text.

### Understanding

- How did Varjak's friends, Holly and Cludge, help Varjak overcome the black cats and get rid of the Gentleman?

- Has Varjak succeeded in his quest even though his family didn't go with him Outside?

- Who was your favourite character apart from Varjak? Give reasons for your choice.

### Inferences

- Were the black cats really evil?

- Would Jalal have been proud of Varjak a) when he first came home and b) by the end of the book?

- Varjak tells Julius there shouldn't be a head of the family and that there must be a better way. What do you think he means?

### Predicting

- Would Jalal have approved of Varjak leaving his family to start a new gang Outside?

- Varjak, Holly and Cludge want to start their own gang. Will their gang be different to the gangs of Sally Bones, Razor and Ginger? Explain your thinking.

### Main ideas

- How did Varjak finally overcome the black cats? Who helped him?

- Where was the Gentleman taking Julius?

- Why did the Gentleman run off? Do you think he has gone for good, as Cludge says?

### Language, structure and presentation

- Is there a difference between 'home' and feeling 'at home'? Explain your thinking.

- What is the significance of 'the sun rising after a long night', just as Varjak tells his family that Outside is where he belongs?

- How does the weather suggest what Varjak's future might be like?

### Themes and conventions

- What did Varjak learn through his adventures? Consider these themes in your answer: nobility, heroism, friendship, loyalty, growing up, being true to yourself.

## SESSION AIMS

Consider how an author introduces the main themes and characters in a novel.

## BEFORE THE SESSION

The children should have read Chapters 1 to 5 before the session.

## READ

- Ask the children to remind themselves of what happens in Chapters 1 to 5.

- Encourage the children to think about all the questions Chapters 1–5 raise. Ask them: *How does the author describe Camp Green Lake? Is it truly a camp? If not, why is it made to sound like one?*

- Consider the character of Stanley Yelnats. Ask: *What does he seem like as a person? What about his family?*

- Ask the children to read Chapter 6 independently. As they read, encourage them to think about what Stanley is accused of. Ask: *Does this seem fair? Does Stanley, like his ancestors, have bad luck? Is the justice system that convicts him fair?*

## REVISIT AND RESPOND

Use the following discussion points to help the children think about what they have read in more depth.

**Note:** Since there are only 20 minutes for each session, you are advised to focus on only one or two of the elements that are listed below.

- Discuss the name 'Camp Green Lake' with the children, especially how it is portrayed at the beginning of Chapter 1. Ask: *Is anything about its name truthful? Is it meant to be ironic?* (Define irony if the children are unsure what it means.) Ask: *Why is it called a 'camp' rather than what it really is?*

- Revisit the section where we discover that Stanley chose to go to Camp Green Lake because he 'was from a poor family. He had never been to camp before'. Observe how Stanley used to pretend he was at a camp, like the rich kids, by using his stuffed animals (cuddly toys). Ask the children: *Do you think Stanley would have chosen Camp Green Lake if he knew the truth?*

- Look at the way in which Stanley is bullied at school. Ask the children: *Why won't the teachers believe that a smaller child could beat up or bully a larger one? Why do children tease their peers because of their weight?* Ask the children to discuss these questions and offer their ideas.

- Next, ask the children if it is possible for teachers to 'make cruel comments without realizing it'. Did the teachers really know they were being unkind to Stanley (after all, they were once children)? Ask: *How would you feel if a teacher made fun of your weight or drew attention to it?* Finally, ask: *Is it equally embarrassing and upsetting for people to make comments about how skinny someone is? Why/why not? Is it more acceptable to be underweight than overweight?*

- Ask the children to consider how the staff at Camp Green Lake are portrayed, particularly Mr Sir and Mr Pendanski. Ask: *Why are they so different in personality and behaviour?* Ask the children to jot down how Mr Sir and Mr Pendanski differ from each other and how that might be related to the jobs they do at the Camp. Next, ask them: *What do you think the Warden is like? Why do we only hear about him through other people? What does it make the reader, and the boys, think the Warden is like?*

- Discuss how the author portrays social justice in these chapters. For example, we hear that the sneakers (trainers) Stanley allegedly 'stole' had belonged to baseball player Clyde Livingston and were going to be auctioned to raise money for a homeless shelter. The potential buyers were rich people who were going to 'pay a hundred dollars to eat the food that the poor people ate every day for free'. Ask the children: *Is it insensitive or patronising for rich people to do that? What do you think the author thinks about this?* Then ask the children to compare this to Stanley's situation – a boy who is too poor to go to camp with rich kids, and whose family could not afford a lawyer (who would probably have freed Stanley). Is the justice system portrayed as fair?

Ask the children, whenever appropriate, to revisit the text to support their answers.

Encourage the children to read aloud back to the group when referring back to the text – praise clear, confident and expressive reading.

## ASSESSMENT OPPORTUNITIES

The following bank of question prompts provides a quick and easy means of monitoring the children's comprehension skills and understanding of the text. The children's answers to a question must be supported by evidence from the text.

### Understanding
- What is so special about Stanley Yelnats' name?
- What does Stanley's father do and what is his latest project?
- How long was the bus trip to the Camp?
- What will Stanley have to wear at the Camp?
- How long will Stanley have to stay at Camp Green Lake?
- What time is breakfast at the Camp, and what do the boys have to do every day?
- What is the name of the outlaw who robbed Stanley's ancestor's stagecoach?

### Inferences
- Why are the boys at Camp Green Lake called 'Campers' when they are not?
- How does Stanley feel when he arrives at the Camp, after his initial expectations?

- Why is Lewis called 'Barf Bag' and why does his bed smell of stale milk?
- Why do the boys insist on having nicknames instead of 'real' names, and why do they call Mr Pendanski 'Mom'?

### Predicting
- Will Stanley be happy at Camp Green Lake?
- Will Stanley ever meet the Warden?

### Language, structure and presentation
- Why is Chapter 2 so short? Why didn't the author include those few paragraphs in Chapter 1 instead? What effect does this have on the book?
- What is a 'barf bag'?
- The first paragraph of Chapter 6 repeats the phrase 'if you could call it that'. Why does the author do this? What is he hoping to achieve?
- What does the word 'suds' mean?
- Look at the language the author uses throughout these chapters. Is it very descriptive? Does it suit the story?

### Themes and conventions
- Does the law treat poorer people unfairly?

# ▼ SESSION 2: LEARNING TO BELONG

## SESSION AIMS

Consider how an author sets a scene through place and characters, and uses flashbacks to develop a story.

## BEFORE THE SESSION

The children should have read Chapters 7 to 10 before the session.

## READ

- Ask the children to remind themselves what happens in Chapters 7 to 10.
- Encourage the children to think about:
  - how Stanley is settling into life at the Camp
  - the way in which the boys behave
  - why they are digging holes every day
  - Elya Yalnets's story and the curse.
- Ask the children to read Chapters 11 to 15. As they read, encourage them to think about:
  - what the boys think about life at the Camp and about their futures
  - why Zero seems like a difficult and unhappy person – why does he get so upset?
  - what the Warden is looking for.

## REVISIT AND RESPOND

Use the following discussion points to help the children think about what they have read in more depth.

**Note:** Since there are only 20 minutes for each session, you are advised to focus on only one or two of the elements that are listed below.

- Refer the children to Chapter 7 and the way in which Stanley's first proper day at Camp Green Lake is interwoven with the tale of his great-great-grandfather, Elya. Ask the children why the author chose to put this story in this chapter rather than

earlier. Do the children like how the author has done this or do they find it disruptive? Ask them: *Is Elya's story as interesting as Stanley's?*

- Looking at Elya's story, ask the children how it could be likened to a fairy or folk tale. (For example, it has a character who has to complete a strange mission a certain amount of times to achieve a goal, and if they don't keep their word a curse may be put on them.) Can the children list any fairy or folk tales they know and say what the main characters have to do? Next, ask the children: *Do you believe in bad luck or curses? Why/why not?* Finally, ask the children if they think that Elya did bring bad luck to his family for not carrying Madame Zeroni to the mountain stream.

- Ask the children to think about how the boys at the Camp are portrayed. Are they like any other boys they know of? Ask them: *Why do the boys insist on being called by their nicknames instead of their normal names? Who decides what nickname a new person should have?* See if the children can suggest reasons why there always has to be a rank or pecking order among children (X-Ray is always seen as the leader and people have to earn their place). Finally, ask: *What is the matter with Zero? Why does he get upset when he sees Stanley's letter? Why is he sullen when Mr Pendanski jokes 'You're not completely worthless' and says 'I like to dig holes'?*

- Can the children suggest why the boys have a negative attitude towards life in general and their lives in particular? For example, why did they damage all the facilities in the Rec (Wreck) Room when they are there for their entertainment? Is it boredom? Anger? Next, explore their discussion with Mr Pendanski and the jokes they make when he encourages them to consider life after Camp Green Lake. Ask: *Why won't the boys be serious about this?*

- Consider how Stanley is being treated at Camp Green Lake compared to his life at school. Ask: *Why does Stanley seem more popular there?*

*Why do the other boys like him? Does Stanley seem happier?* Refer the children to the end of Chapter 11 when Stanley finds digging his hole easier, imagining the boys at Camp beating up his enemy Derrick. Ask the children: *Will Stanley's experience at the Camp boost his self-confidence? Will it be good for him?*

- Revisit Chapters 14 and 15, when the Warden appears. Ask the children: *Were you expecting the Warden to be female? Why/why not? Why did the author keep her gender a secret until now?*

- Ask the children to look at how Mr Pendanski reacts to the Warden and how she treats him. Ask: *Why does she behave more kindly to the children and harder on Mr Pendanski? Why does she use their nicknames?*

Ask the children, whenever appropriate, to revisit the text to exemplify/support their answers.

Encourage the children to read aloud back to the group when referring back to the text – praise clear, confident and expressive reading.

## ASSESSMENT OPPORTUNITIES

The following bank of question prompts provides a quick and easy means of monitoring the children's comprehension skills and understanding of the text. The children's answers to a question must be supported by evidence from the text.

### Understanding
- How long were the shovels?
- Where was Stanley's great-great-grandfather from?
- What did Myra's father want to swap her for?
- Who is always at the front of the water queue?
- What did Stanley find that he thought would interest the Warden?
- What initials were carved on the gold tube?

### Inferences
- What 'interesting' thing is the Warden looking for?
- How would Myra have felt to be worth as much as a fat pig?

- Why does Mr Sir keep talking about the Girl Scouts to Stanley?
- Why do the boys spit into their hole when they have finished digging?
- What will Stanley do, now that he knows there is something special the Warden is searching for?

### Predicting
- Will Stanley be more self-confident now?
- Will Stanley find something interesting?

### Language, structure and presentation
- What is a 'canteen' in this story?
- What is a 'baloney sandwich'? What are 'potato chips'?
- Why is Chapter 8 only about yellow-spotted lizards? Is this important for the story?
- What is a Rec Room? And why have the boys changed it to Wreck Room?

### Themes and conventions
- How are friendships made in difficult circumstances?
- Is it possible to be successful after a bad start in life?

# ▼ SESSION 3: TAKING THE BLAME

## SESSION AIMS

Infer how a story might develop from what characters say and do.

## BEFORE THE SESSION

The children should have read Chapters 15 to 19 before the session.

## READ

- Ask the children to remind themselves of what happens in Chapters 15 to 19, while thinking about:
  - how the boys' characters are slowly developing
  - how desperate the Warden is to find something, and what this might be
  - why Stanley takes the blame for the sunflower seeds.
- Ask the children to read Chapters 20 to 22 independently. As they read, encourage them to pay special attention to:
  - why the Warden punishes Mr Sir instead of Stanley
  - how Zero knows so much about Stanley.

## REVISIT AND RESPOND

Use the following discussion points to help the children think about what they have read in more depth.

**Note:** Since there are only 20 minutes for each session, you are advised to focus on only one or two of the elements that are listed below.

- Revisit Chapter 15, where the boys tell Stanley that the Warden has tiny cameras hidden all over the place, including the showers. Ask the children: *Why do you think she has done this? What do you think she is hoping to find out?* Then ask the children whether they think this kind of behaviour is legal. Ask: *Is this an invasion of privacy? If so, are*

*'prisoners' allowed privacy?* Ask the children to explain their views. Finish by asking the children how they would feel if there were cameras like this in their school, including the toilets. Ask them: *What would you do? What would you say about it, and to whom?* (The children's responses could be played out as a drama or public speaking activity, with one side for cameras and one side against.)

- When Stanley receives a letter from his mother, the other boys tease him. Ask the children: *Why do you think the boys do this? Do you think the other boys get letters from their parents? Are they jealous?* Ask: *Why does X-Ray help Stanley by telling the others to back off, and that the letter was probably from Stanley's girlfriend?*

- Next, look at the news that Stanley's mother shares. Ask the children: *Do you think that Stanley's father should get a job that pays rather than keeping his family in financial hardship?*

- Revisit Chapter 18 where Zero asks Stanley to teach him how to read and write, and Stanley refuses because 'His heart had hardened as well [as his body].' Ask the children: *Is it good that Stanley has become more hard-hearted? Did he need to in order to survive at the Camp?* Ask the children if they think Stanley will turn into the sort of boy who used to bully him at school now that he is quite popular at the Camp. Should Stanley know better? Finally, ask the children how hard it would have been for Zero to admit to Stanley that he could not read or write. Ask them: *How can a child get to that age and not know how to read or write? And why does Zero have no one to write to?*

- In Chapter 20, Mr Sir takes Stanley to the Warden because he doesn't believe Stanley stole his sunflower seeds but thinks he is covering up for the thief or thieves. Ask the children: *Why bother the Warden with this? What did Mr Sir think would happen as a result?* Next, ask the children if they expected the Warden to react as she did. Why did she punish Mr Sir instead of Stanley, and why so severely? Finally, ask: *What does the Warden mean when she says that Mr Sir won't die, 'Unfortunately for you'. What does this mean for Stanley?*

- Ask the children why Zero dug Stanley's hole, especially after Stanley refused to help him before. Ask: *Why didn't the other boys help, since Stanley had covered up for them and Zero hadn't even eaten the seeds? Is this what finally persuades Stanley to help Zero?* Ask the children to look at the first lesson Stanley gives Zero, when he discovers Zero's gift for maths. Zero says he's not stupid; he just doesn't like answering people. Why is this?

Ask the children, whenever appropriate, to revisit the text to exemplify/support their answers.

Encourage the children to read aloud back to the group when referring back to the text – praise clear, confident and expressive reading.

## ASSESSMENT OPPORTUNITIES

The following bank of question prompts provides a quick and easy means of monitoring the children's comprehension skills and understanding of the text. The children's answers to a question must be supported by evidence from the text.

### Understanding
- Which three authors does Stanley think about?
- Which nursery rhyme is mentioned in these chapters?
- How heavy was the sack of sunflower seeds?
- How did the Warden injure Mr Sir?
- Who found Stanley's great-grandfather in the desert?
- Where had Stanley seen the initials KB before?

### Inferences
- Why wouldn't Squid admit to crying?
- Why did Stanley cover for the other boys?
- Why didn't the Warden punish Stanley? Does she like Mr Sir?

### Predicting
- What will Mr Sir do to Stanley for revenge, if anything?
- Will Zero and Stanley become good friends?

### Main ideas
- How has Stanley changed since the start of the story? Is this for the better?

### Language, structure and presentation
- The first paragraph in Chapter 20 likens the way Stanley walks to the Warden's house to that of a condemned man walking to his death. Does this help increase the suspense at what will happen to Stanley?
- What is a rattlesnake?
- What is 'Sesame Street'?
- What does 'writhing' mean?
- What kind of picture is the author presenting of the Warden from these chapters?

### Themes and conventions
- Should you always take the blame for your friends?
- Is it bad to tell tales on someone, no matter what your age?

# SESSION 4: KISSING KATE BARLOW

## SESSION AIMS

Discuss whether authors express their own views in a story and, if so, how they do this.

## BEFORE THE SESSION

The children should have read Chapters 23 to 26 before the session.

## READ

- Ask the children to remind themselves of what happens in Chapters 23 to 26, while thinking about:
  - what it would have been like living in Texas 110 years ago and how society differed to nowadays.
  - how and why Katherine Barlow became an outlaw
  - Mr Sir's treatment of Stanley.
- Continue the session by asking the children to read Chapters 27 and 28 independently. As they read, they should think about:
  - whether Stanley's view of X-Ray and the other boys is changing – and whether his own self-confidence is growing
  - the significance of Zero's real name
  - who the Warden is
  - how what the boys are doing relates to Katherine Barlow's legacy.

## REVISIT AND RESPOND

Use the following discussion points to help the children think about what they have read in more depth.

**Note:** Since there are only 20 minutes for each session, you are advised to focus on only one or two of the elements that are listed below.

- Ask the children to look at the way in which the people of Green Lake treat Sam the onion seller. Ask: *Is he liked? Is he trusted? If so, why is he not allowed to attend classes at the local school? When Sam fixes the schoolhouse, do the people thank*

him or take the credit themselves? Explain to the children that, although the author makes no direct comment on how Sam is treated, sometimes the reader can guess. Ask: *What do you think the author's views are on Sam's treatment? Can you find any examples to support your opinion?*

- Consider how the people of Green Lake respond to Sam and Katherine's kiss. Ask the children: *Why do they bring God into their response?* For example, one person says 'God will punish you' and Trout Walker calls Katherine 'The Devil Woman'. Do the children think that God would punish people of different colours or races for falling in love? Ask them: *Why is it legal for Katherine to kiss Sam but not the other way around? Is this fair?* Next, ask the children: *Why do the townspeople now think that Katherine has been poisoning their children's minds? Why do they burn the books? Do the children think that the people assume the books have corrupted Katherine?*

- Look at what the author says at the end of Chapter 26, when the author directly talks to the reader after telling them that, after Sam's murder, the town never saw a drop of rain for 110 years: 'You make the decision: Whom did God punish?' Ask the children: *Did God punish anyone? Or is it just coincidence? Does the author believe God did this or is he using God because that is what the townspeople do?* Do the children believe that, if there is a God, he or she would be vengeful and get involved with people's battles?

- In Chapter 28, Katherine is now Kate. Ask the children why her name has now been shortened: *Is it to differentiate her as an outlaw? If so, could she not have chosen a completely different name?* Next, look at the section where Kate tells Trout that he will have to dig to find the buried loot: 'You, and your children, and their children, can dig for the next hundred years and you'll never find it'. Ask the children: *Does the main story, in the present day, now make sense to you? Who do you think the Warden is, now you have this information? Do you think she will ever find the treasure?*

In Chapter 27, the boys comment on how Zero is helping Stanley dig his hole, and X-Ray doesn't like it. '[Stanley] knew X-Ray wouldn't have been talking like that if *he* was the one teaching Zero to read… [he'd] be talking about how important it was that he got his rest, *right*?' Ask the children: *Is Stanley's attitude towards X-Ray and the other boys changing? Why is this, when he used to be grateful for X-Ray's support? Is Stanley becoming more self-confident?*

Ask the children, whenever appropriate, to revisit the text to exemplify/support their answers.

Encourage the children to read aloud back to the group when referring back to the text – praise clear, confident and expressive reading.

## ASSESSMENT OPPORTUNITIES

The following bank of question prompts provides a quick and easy means of monitoring the children's comprehension skills and understanding of the text. The children's answers to a question must be supported by evidence from the text.

### Understanding
- What did Katherine always win a prize for?
- Why was Charles Walker called 'Trout'?
- What was the name of the onion seller?
- For how many years was Kate an outlaw?
- Who did Trout Walker marry and how did Kate know her?
- How did Kate die?

### Inferences
- Why does Mr Sir hurt the boy who asks what happened to his face?
- Why does the woman think that God will punish Kate for kissing Sam?
- Why does Kate become an outlaw? Why does she kiss the Sheriff after killing him?
- Why doesn't Mr Sir give Stanley water at first? When he does, what does Stanley think he has put in it?

### Predicting
- Is Zero – Hector Zeroni – a relative of Madame Zeroni? What might this mean to the story?
- Is there any treasure buried at Camp Green Lake?

### Language, structure and presentation
- What does the word 'grotesque' mean?
- Why does the author choose to split the story from the past between chapters of the story in the present, rather than do it all in one chapter as he did earlier with Elya's story? Which method do you prefer?
- What is a mob?
- What is loot?

### Themes and conventions
- Consider how racial inequality is portrayed in the story and what the author might be trying to say.

# ▼ SESSION 5: ESCAPE

## SESSION AIMS

Consider how an author builds tension and suspense in a story through the way the characters behave.

## BEFORE THE SESSION

The children should have read Chapters 29 to 31 before the session.

## READ

- Ask the children to remind themselves of what happens in Chapters 29 to 31. They should think about:
  - what caused the fight between the boys
  - why Mr Pendanski is so unkind to Zero
  - why Zero has changed the way he thinks, now he's been friends with Stanley.
- Ask the children to read Chapters 32 to 34 independently. As they read, encourage them to think about:
  - why Stanley decides to risk his life and go after Zero
  - why Stanley didn't plan his escape more.

## REVISIT AND RESPOND

Use the following discussion points to help the children think about what they have read in more depth.

**Note:** Since there are only 20 minutes for each session, you are advised to focus on only one or two of the elements that are listed below.

- In Chapter 30, the boys start being more aggressive towards Stanley, accusing Stanley of thinking that he is better than the rest of them. Ask the children: *What has caused this change of feeling towards Stanley, and why? Does Stanley think he is better than the other boys?* Ask the children to consider the boys reporting Zero for digging Stanley's hole. Ask: *Why did they this do this when Stanley took*

the blame for the sunflower seeds? Is this fair? Should Stanley dig his own hole? Does he need rest in order to teach?*

- Ask the children to look at how Mr Pendanski behaves in Chapter 30. Ask: *Why does Mr Pendanski encourage Stanley to hit Zigzag back, to 'teach the bully a lesson'? Is this what a teacher should do? Is using violence against violence a good thing?* Next, ask the children to consider 'why Mr Pendanski seemed to have it in for Zero', for example when he says 'He's so stupid, he doesn't even know he's stupid'. Ask: *Why is Mr Pendanski so horrible about Zero? Does he know something we don't?* Then consider Zero's response to Mr Pendanski's insults. Ask the children: *Did Mr Pendanski deserve being hit in the face with the shovel? Why does Zero now say: 'I hate digging holes'?*

- Look at the part in Chapter 30 where the Warden forbids Stanley to teach Zero how to read or write anymore because 'It leads to trouble'. Ask: *Do the children agree with the Warden's view here? Does education lead to trouble? Why/why not?* Ask the children to link this section to earlier in the book, when the townspeople burnt the books in the schoolhouse after Katherine Barlow kissed Sam. Ask: *Is this similar to what the Warden is saying? Is education dangerous?*

- In Chapter 31, the Warden, Mr Sir and Mr Pendanski wait for Stanley to return from digging his hole. Ask the children: *Why are they so keen to know as much as possible about Zero? Why do they think that Stanley would know so much? Why does the Warden want all his records deleted from their systems and any others that they can access? Isn't this suspicious?* Finally, ask: *What does the Warden mean when she says 'He was never here'?*

- Ask the children: *Was Stanley brave to try to go off to rescue Zero or was he silly not to have planned it better? Was it bad luck that Stanley drove the truck into a hole?* Next, ask the children to discuss, in pairs, how they would have done things differently to Stanley; they should share answers as a group.

- Ask what sort of atmosphere the author has created in these chapters – does it feel tenser now than before? If so, how has the author achieved this tension?

Ask the children, whenever appropriate, to revisit the text to exemplify/support their answers.

Encourage the children to read aloud back to the group when referring back to the text – praise clear, confident and expressive reading.

## ASSESSMENT OPPORTUNITIES

The following bank of question prompts provides a quick and easy means of monitoring the children's comprehension skills and understanding of the text. The children's answers to a question must be supported by evidence from the text.

### Understanding

- Why doesn't the truck move at first?
- When are the mountains visible to Stanley and why?
- How long has Stanley been at Camp Green Lake?
- Where are the guards stationed to stop Zero?
- Where was Zero living before he was arrested?
- What is the name of the new boy?
- What was the name of the old boat on the lake?

### Inferences

- Why did Mr Sir give Zizag an extra carton of juice?
- Why does all the food come in a can at Camp Green Lake?
- Would Zero have killed Zigzag?
- Stanley looks into the holes beyond the Camp but 'didn't want to admit what he was looking for'. What was he looking for?

### Predicting

- Will Stanley and Zero survive in the heat without water?
- Will anyone come to look for them?

### Language, structure and presentation

- What does 'humid' mean?
- What does 'to have it in for someone' mean?
- Chapter 30 is quite a long chapter in this book. Why do you think Chapter 30 is longer than some of the other chapters?
- In Chapter 31 the author keeps repeating 'It wasn't impossible'? Why? What is the effect of this?
- What is 'a ward of the state'?
- What is a mirage?

### Themes and conventions

- How far would you be prepared to go for a friend?
- If someone hits you, is it right for you to hit that person back?

# ▼ SESSION 6: TRIUMPH OVER ADVERSITY

## SESSION AIMS

Consider how the themes in one book are similar to those in other books the children might have read.

## BEFORE THE SESSION

The children should have read Chapters 35 to 38 before the session.

## READ

- Ask the children to remind themselves of what happens in Chapters 35 to 38, while thinking about:
  - the boys' journey towards the mountains and what keeps them going
  - what's wrong with Zero and whether he will get better
  - Zero's determination not to give up and Stanley's devotion to him.
- Ask the children to read Chapters 39 and 40 independently. As they read, they should think about:
  - whether the boys will survive on the mountain
  - the link between the boys' situation and what happened there 110 years ago
  - the story of Elya Yelnats.

## REVISIT AND RESPOND

Use the following discussion points to help the children think about what they have read in more depth.

**Note:** Since there are only 20 minutes for each session, you are advised to focus on only one or two of the elements that are listed below.

- In Chapter 36, the boys wonder who Mary Lou is and assume she must have been a woman to have a boat named after her. Stanley says: 'I bet she looked great in a bathing suit'. Ask the children: *Can you remember who the boat is named after?* (Mary Lou,

Sam's donkey.) *Is this funny?* Ask the children why Sam named his boat after his donkey. Finally, ask if they can think of any other boats named after women in real life or in books.

- In Chapter 36, Stanley is not worried about pain or dying but 'the thought of his parents not knowing what happened to him, not knowing whether he was dead or alive… the pain would never end.' Ask the children what this means and to discuss, in pairs, whether it is more worrying to die or to think about the ones you love and how they will cope. The children could extend this by role-playing the situation where Stanley's parents receive news of their son's disappearance or death.

- Ask the children to look at the opening of Chapter 38, where it says that Stanley's 'strength came from somewhere deep inside himself and also seemed to come from the outside as well… it was as if the rock had absorbed his energy and now acted like a kind of giant magnet pulling him toward it…' Ask: *What does this mean? What is this energy and is it possible to get energy from something else?* Next, ask them if this situation reminds them of Elya's climb to the top of the mountain. Ask: *Is Stanley's situation meant to be similar to Elya's?*

- Does Stanley's achievement remind the children of any other books they have read, where a person triumphs over adversity or succeeds in a near-impossible quest. Can they give any examples (for example, Harry Potter, *Lord of the Rings*)?

- Ask the children to consider the way in which Chapter 40 is structured, with a flashback to Sam the onion seller saving a young girl's life sandwiched between Stanley finding the onion plants and the boys eating them. Ask the children: *Why did the author structure the chapter like this? What might he be trying to suggest?*

- Ask the children to consider what Sam did and whether the Tennysons should have stood up for him when the other townspeople were persecuting him. If he saved their daughter's life, why wouldn't they help save his?

- At the end of Chapter 40, Stanley can't believe how he managed to climb with Zero on his back when he was so weak. Ask the children: *How did Stanley do it? Do they think this is similar to what Stanley's ancestor, Elya Yelnats, did?*

Ask the children, whenever appropriate, to revisit the text to exemplify/support their answers.

Encourage the children to read aloud back to the group when referring back to the text – praise clear, confident and expressive reading.

## ASSESSMENT OPPORTUNITIES

The following bank of question prompts provides a quick and easy means of monitoring the children's comprehension skills and understanding of the text. The children's answers to a question must be supported by evidence from the text.

### Understanding
- What is the 'sploosh' that Zero and Stanley are drinking?
- What do Zero and Stanley pretend was on top of Big Thumb?
- What did Stanley find in the mud to eat?
- Where did Stanley wake up?
- What did Zero confess to doing?

### Inferences
- Why does the spelling help Zero when the two boys are walking?
- Why is Zero's smile 'clown-like'?
- How hard must it be for Zero to keep walking and climbing?
- Why does Stanley tell Zero that the onion is a 'hot fudge sundae'?

### Predicting
- Will Zero recover?
- Will the boys get off the mountain? If they do, where will they go?

### Language, structure and presentation
- What is a 'jack-o'-lantern'?
- What does 'it was like chasing the moon' mean?
- What are 'gnats'?
- What is the UK English word for 'bugs'?
- What does 'contritely' mean?
- In Chapter 8, the sentence 'You need water to make mud' is in italics – why?
- What does 'delirious' mean?

### Themes and conventions
- Look at how the author portrays the boys' ascent of Big Thumb. Can you think of any other books that have a similar theme of carrying on in the face of adversity?
- Consider the importance of never giving up, even when everything seems impossible.

**SESSION 7:** ZERO'S STORY

## SESSION AIMS

Consider how important themes such as homelessness and stealing for necessity, rather than greed, are portrayed in the book.

## BEFORE THE SESSION

The children should have read Chapters 41 and 42 before the session.

## READ

- Ask the children to remind themselves of what happens in Chapters 41 and 42, while thinking about:
  - Zero's childhood story and what it must have been like to be homeless at such a young age, especially when his mother disappeared
  - how destiny, fate and/or coincidence brought the two boys together – was it an accident or was it something that was meant to happen?
  - whether the boys will get off the mountain and, if they do, where they will go.
- Ask the children to read Chapter 43 independently. As they read, they should think about:
  - the boys' journey back to Camp Green Lake and how it differs from their escape
  - why Stanley's happiness turns to fear as he gets closer to the Camp – is it nerves or something else?

## REVISIT AND RESPOND

Use the following discussion points to help the children think about what they have read in more depth.

**Note:** Since there are only 20 minutes for each session, you are advised to focus on only one or two of the elements that are listed below.

- In Chapter 41, the reader hears Zero's story of homelessness before he arrived at Camp Green Lake. Ask the children to list the sort of things Zero experienced, both with his mother and without

her, and to discuss how he must have felt. Ask: *Would Zero have been scared while he was with his mother? How did he feel when she disappeared and he had to survive on his own? How did he manage at such a young age to feed himself and get shelter? Why not ask for help?*

- Refer the children to Chapter 43, in which Zero describes an incident in a park at a children's birthday party. Ask: *How do the children react to him? Why does the mother shoo him away when one of the children offers him cake? Was this a kind thing to do?*

- In Chapter 41, Zero talks about how he and his mother 'always took what we needed… never more', and that he didn't know that behaving that way was stealing. Ask the children: *Is stealing bad if you are hungry or need food and have no money? Is stealing worse if you take things when you don't need them?*

- Look at Zero's explanation of how he came across Clyde Livingston's shoes and how he thought it was better to take old, used shoes than new ones. Do the children agree with Zero? Ask them: *Was Zero's decision a moral one?* Ask the children whether they can think of other stories in which people steal for 'good' reasons or because of necessity (for example, *Oliver Twist*, *Robin Hood*).

- Consider how Zero's and Stanley's stories link together in Chapter 42. Stanley thinks this is destiny – do the children agree? (If the children do not understand this concept/belief, provide an explanation of destiny and link it to the idea of fate). Ask the children: *Do you believe that we decide how our lives go ourselves, or do things happen to us that are not under our control?* Encourage the children to discuss this idea and then share ideas.

- Read the short section, near the beginning of Chapter 42, from '[Stanley] was too happy to fall asleep' to 'He liked himself now'. Ask the children: *Why is Stanley so happy after all he has been through? Would you feel happy if you were Stanley?* Next, ask the children what it means when Stanley thinks: 'It occurred to him that he couldn't remember the last time he felt happiness'? Ask: *Why has Stanley been so unhappy all his life? Why does he feel better about himself now? Why didn't he like himself before?*

Ask the children, whenever appropriate, to revisit the text to exemplify/support their answers.

Encourage the children to read aloud back to the group when referring back to the text – praise clear, confident and expressive reading.

## ASSESSMENT OPPORTUNITIES

The following bank of question prompts provides a quick and easy means of monitoring the children's comprehension skills and understanding of the text. The children's answers to a question must be supported by evidence from the text.

### Understanding

- Why do the boys wash their socks away from the water hole?
- How many onions have Stanley and Zero eaten since they have been on Big Thumb?
- What colour was Zero's room when he was young?
- What was the name of Zero's stuffed animal, and what type of animal was it?
- How do the boys compete on their journey back to the Camp?

### Inferences

- Why doesn't Stanley get sick from the sploosh?
- If Clyde Livingston's shoes are too small for Stanley's feet, what does this mean about his guilt or innocence? Why wasn't this checked at the trial?
- Why doesn't Stanley want to say the word 'homeless' to Zero? Why does he say 'moved out' instead?

### Predicting

- Will the boys find Kate Barlow's buried treasure?
- Where will they go afterwards if they are not caught?
- What will happen to the boys if they are caught?

### Main ideas

- What is the author saying about destiny in the book?

### Language, structure and presentation

- Look at Chapter 41, where Zero talks about taking food that they need. Why is the word 'stealing' in italics?
- What does the word 'destiny' mean?
- At the end of Chapter 42, there are two statements in italics. Why has the author chosen to do this?
- Look at the diagram in Chapter 43. Does it help the story to have this in? Is it needed or not? Do you like it?
- Why does the author tell Zero's story in small parts, throughout the different chapters, rather than in one larger piece?

### Themes and conventions

- How does the author convey homelessness in the story?

# SESSION 8: FILLING THE HOLES

## SESSION AIMS

Consider how the author brings together all aspects of the story and reveals how the main characters have developed as a result of what has happened to them.

## BEFORE THE SESSION

The children should have read Chapters 44 to 49 before the session.

## READ

- Ask the children to remind themselves of what happens in Chapters 44 to 49, while thinking about:
  - what happened with the lizards when the boys were in the hole – why weren't Stanley and Zero harmed?
  - whether the staff at Camp Green Lake all knew about the real treasure the Warden was looking for.
- Ask the children to read Chapter 50 independently. As they read, the children should think about:
  - how all the different stories in the book finally come together, and how they link the main characters
  - how the boys' lives will be different from now on.

## REVISIT AND RESPOND

Use the following discussion points to help the children think about what they have read in more depth.

**Note:** Since there are only 20 minutes for each session, you are advised to focus on only one or two of the elements that are listed below.

- At the end of Chapter 45, the Warden talks about her childhood, saying: 'When I was little I'd watch my parents dig holes every weekend and holiday. When I got bigger, I had to dig too. Even on Christmas.' Ask the children to think about who she is and how her past ties in with Stanley's. Does she know their link? Then ask: *What would it have been*

*like for her to grow up the way she did? Do you feel sorry for the Warden now?*

- Looking at Chapters 49 and 50, ask the children how the various stories in the novel come together: Elya's and Madame Zeroni's, Kate's and Sam's, and Stanley's and Zero's. Ask: *Do you think it is clever how the author has weaved together these three stories from the past and present? Does what the author has done work or is it confusing? Which story do you prefer and why?* Ask the children whether they think there really was a curse on Stanley's family, bearing in mind what the author says when he addresses 'The reader'. When giving their answers, encourage the children to make specific links to the text.

- Ask the children whether the lizards play an important part in the story. Rather than threatening their lives, do they save Stanley and Zero from the staff? Ask: *If the lizards hadn't been there in the hole, would the staff have shot the boys? What protected the boys, in the end, from the lizards?*

- Ask the children if they think all the staff knew exactly what the Warden was looking for. Would she have shared her treasure with them? If not, then what would they have done to her?

- Revisit the paragraph towards the end of Chapter 50 where we see Zero (now always called 'Hector') with his mother. Ask the children to discuss why she looks different – what do the descriptions tell them about the time she has been through since the two last met? Ask them to consider how the two might have been reunited and to role-play the conversation between them. Ask: *What questions would Zero and his mother ask each other, and what answers would they give? How would they have felt?*

- Ask the children to share their views about the book as a whole. Do they feel justice has been done, especially since Stanley was wrongly convicted but did not seem to receive any compensation for this? Ask: *How has this experience changed Stanley's life? Was it good for him despite (or because of) the hardships he faced? How has he benefited, apart from the money?*

Ask the children, whenever appropriate, to revisit the text to exemplify/support their answers.

Encourage the children to read aloud back to the group when referring back to the text – praise clear, confident and expressive reading.

## ASSESSMENT OPPORTUNITIES

The following bank of question prompts provides a quick and easy means of monitoring the children's comprehension skills and understanding of the text. The children's answers to a question must be supported by evidence from the text.

### Understanding

- What does Zero bring Stanley for breakfast when they return to the Camp?
- What is Mr Sir wearing by the hole?
- How many lizards can Stanley count in the hole?
- What is the name of Stanley's lawyer?
- What key ingredient makes up Stanley's father's 'sploosh' treatment? What does the sploosh do?
- How much money do Stanley and Hector each receive? How do they spend it?

### Inferences

- Why does the Warden wait until the boys have dug the hole to reveal herself? Why does she wear boots?
- Why is standing very still for a long time more tiring than walking?
- Why do the boys smell very bad?
- Why is it significant that a drop of rain finally falls on the dried-up lake after the boys leave the Camp?
- Why does the author refer to Zero as 'Hector' throughout Chapter 50, rather than by his nickname?

### Predicting

- Will Stanley's father continue to do well?
- Will Zero and his mother be able to live together now?
- Will Stanley and Zero ever see the other boys again?

### Language, structure and presentation

- What is a tarantula?
- What is an 'attorney'? What does 'jurisdiction' mean?
- What does the author mean when he says: '[Ms Moreno] was shorter than Stanley but gave the appearance of being tall'?
- In Chapter 49, why does the author include the short flashback to Sam selling onions to rattlesnake hunters?
- Why is Part 3 so short? And what does its title 'Filling in the Holes' mean?

### Themes and conventions

- Is this story like a fairy tale? Explain your thinking.

**SESSION 1:** PLANS

## SESSION AIMS

Predict what might happen.

## BEFORE THE SESSION

The children should have read Chapter 1 prior to the session.

## READ

- Ask the children to talk to a partner about what has happened in the story so far and to scan Chapter 1 independently to remind themselves of recent events.

- Involve the children in a brief group discussion. Ask them:

  - How did the rats change and become educated?

  - What is the town that Maurice, Keith and the rats are now near?

  - What is the trick that Maurice, Keith and the rats agree to play on the town?

- Ask the children: *Does it seem likely that Maurice will keep to his agreement with Keith and the rats?* Then ask them to read Chapter 2 independently, keeping this type of question in mind.

### During reading

- Ask the children to think about the information and the questions that arise for them as they read.

- If your school uses reading journals then the children should be encouraged to make notes as they read and consider each question.

- Move around the group and 'tune in' to hear individuals read aloud. Encourage and praise good expression.

## REVISIT AND RESPOND

Use the following discussion points to help the children think about what they have read in more depth.

**Note:** Since there are only 20 minutes for each session, you are advised to focus on only one or two of the elements that are listed below.

- Ask the children to consider the morality of the trick played on towns. Ask them: *Should Maurice have used his 'amazing idea'? Did he persuade Keith and the rats to behave badly? Were the rats just doing what was necessary to realise their dream of establishing an island civilisation? Is the trick harmless fun?* What arguments can the children make for and against the trick?

- Examine the relationship between Maurice and Dangerous Beans in Chapter 1. How do they feel about each other? How do they treat each other? Is there mutual trust and respect? Ask the children to discuss and list the different strengths and weaknesses of the two characters.

- Direct the children to the final three pages of Chapter 1. Ask them to re-read them and put themselves in the place of Maurice, Keith or one of the rats. How do they feel as the meeting ends?

- Hold a group discussion on the perceptiveness of Maurice when he first enters the town in Chapter 2. As the children provide information, write a list on the whiteboard of what Maurice notices. Which of these things do the children think would have been obvious to them?

- Direct the children to the first mention of 'a girl' in Chapter 2. Explore the character created by the author. Ask the children: *How much does she speak? What unusual things does she say? Why does she talk about a 'wizard', 'cauldron' and 'magical'?* Do the children think that the girl will be an important character later on?

- Examine how much information the author has supplied by the end of Chapter 2. Concentrate on some of the main characters or the town, Bad Blintz. The children should identify what they now know and what they still want to find out about the characters or place. (Activity 2 on page 25 of *Read and Respond The Amazing Maurice and His Educated Rodents* could be a useful guide here.)

- Question the children about the function of Chapter 1. Ask them: *Does the chapter satisfy the requirements for a beginning? Does the chapter finish well? Why?* Would the children have ended the chapter at a different place or in a different way? Share ideas.

- Comment that dialogue is important in Chapter 2. Let the children re-read some conversations between Maurice and Keith. Ask: *What do their conversations reveal about the characters' feelings towards each other?*

- Share predictions about what might happen in Chapter 3.

Ask the children, whenever appropriate, to revisit the text to exemplify/support their answers.

Encourage the children to read aloud back to the group when referring back to the text – praise clear, confident and expressive reading.

## ASSESSMENT OPPORTUNITIES

The following bank of question prompts provides a quick and easy means of monitoring the children's comprehension skills and understanding of the text. The children's answers to a question must be supported by evidence from the text.

### Understanding
- What musical instrument does Keith play?
- What is strange about the market stalls in Bad Blintz?
- What does the sign offer money for?
- What is suspicious about the rat-catcher's boots?
- What is different about the Mayor of this town?
- What does Maurice work out about food here?

### Inferences
- Why is Maurice angry that people are listening to Keith's music?
- Why does reading about the reward of 50 pence a tail make Maurice cheerful?

- Why is it an insult when Maurice washes himself near the rat-catcher's dog?
- How does Keith feel when the rat-catcher pats him on the back?
- Does Maurice want to be sold to the man and leave Keith?

### Predicting
- Will Maurice's plan succeed in Bad Blintz?
- Will Maurice let Keith have a peaceful life playing his flute in the future?

### Main ideas
- Is Maurice happy at the end of the Chapter 2? Why?
- Consider Keith's life. Is Maurice a suitable friend for him?

### Language, structure and presentation
- Re-read the chapter heading preceding Chapter 2. Does it make an important contribution to the chapter? How does it relate to the story's plot?
- What do Maurice and Keith's conversations reveal about the characters' feelings towards each other?
- What is a 'rathaus' (on the notice in Chapter 2)? What language is the word? What does it tell you about the story?
- Why is 'krllrrt' in italics in the last few pages of Chapter 1? How is Hamnpork saying the word? What does Maurice know about the word?

# ▼ SESSION 2: CONFUSION

## SESSION AIMS

Consider language and its impact on the reader.

## BEFORE THE SESSION

The children should have read Chapter 3 prior to the session.

## READ

- Ask the children to talk to a partner about what has happened in the story so far and to scan Chapter 3 independently, to remind themselves of recent events.

- Then involve the children in a brief group discussion. Ask them:

  - Why does Darktan wear belts?
  - What does Hamnpork feel about candles?
  - Why does Hamnpork remind the others frequently that he is the leader?

- Ask the children: *What words does the author use in Chapter 3 to describe Dangerous Beans, Darktan and Peaches so that the reader begins to understand their different personalities?* Then ask them to read Chapter 4 independently, keeping this question in mind.

### During reading

- Ask the children to think about the information and the questions that arise for them as they read.

- If your school uses reading journals then the children should be encouraged to make notes as they read and consider each question.

- Move around the group and 'tune in' to hear individuals read aloud. Encourage and praise good expression.

## REVISIT AND RESPOND

Use the following discussion points to help the children think about what they have read in more depth.

**Note:** Since there are only 20 minutes for each session, you are advised to focus on only one or two of the elements that are listed below.

- Write 'Hamnpork' on the whiteboard. Ask: *What is the name short for?* (Ham and pork.) *How do you react to reading or hearing the name? Which other rat names are surprising?* Share reactions to reading, saying and hearing them. What impact do the children think the author wanted to have on the reader?

- Get the children to carry out a character study of Hamnpork. What are the main characteristics that he reveals in Chapter 3? As the children put forward ideas, list them on the board. Discuss which characteristics are strengths and which are weaknesses.

- Direct the children to the end of Chapter 2 to re-read. Explain that Chapter 4 returns to this story point. Can the children explain the rat problem that the town has? Share ideas on whether Maurice is pleased or disappointed to learn this.

- Point out that, towards the end of Chapter 4, Maurice decides that Malicia is 'making up a story about it'. What does Maurice mean? Do the children think that Maurice is correct? What has Malicia done or said so far in Chapter 4 that leads to this conclusion?

- Investigate the early conversation in Chapter 4. Which character(s) seem to do most of the talking? How do Malicia and Maurice react to each other? Ask the children to put themselves in Maurice's place. Ask them: *How would you feel about Malicia? What would you ask her?*

- Suggest to the children that Keith, early in Chapter 4, does more observing than speaking. What do the children think he notices or thinks? The children could use a hot-seat situation, one child taking the role of Keith with the others in the group questioning him (you could base this on Activity 1 on page 32 of *Read and Respond The Amazing Maurice and His Educated Rodents*).

- Let the children put themselves into the situation by bringing the events of Chapter 4 to life in a series of tableaux or freeze-frames. (You could use the format described in Activity 4 on page 33 of *Read and Respond The Amazing Maurice and His Educated Rodents*.) Encourage the children to step out of their tableau and speak their character's thoughts.

Ask the children, whenever appropriate, to revisit the text to exemplify/support their answers.

Encourage the children to read aloud back to the group when referring back to the text – praise clear, confident and expressive reading.

## ASSESSMENT OPPORTUNITIES

The following bank of question prompts provides a quick and easy means of monitoring the children's comprehension skills and understanding of the text. The children's answers to a question must be supported by evidence from the text.

### Understanding
- Why does Malicia wear a large key to a metal box?
- What position does Malicia's father have?
- What does Malicia expect Maurice to laugh at?
- What did Sardines pull out of his knapsack?
- Where does Sardines get stuck?

### Inferences
- Why does Maurice try to stop Keith telling the truth?
- What does Malicia mean when she says 'That's not how it should go'?
- Why is Maurice surprised when Keith tells Malicia his name?
- What makes Keith tell Malicia so much about himself?
- Does Malicia claim that her aunts wrote better fairy tales than the usual ones?

### Predictions
- What does Malicia predict will happen if she tells anyone she has been talking to a rat and a cat?
- What might happen in Chapter 5? Will the setting change?

### Main ideas
- Is Maurice's plan going well? What worrying incidents have occurred? Are events getting out of control?
- Is Malicia a dangerous character to be involved with? Why?

### Language, structure and presentation
- Point out that Chapter 4 contains a new setting. Where are the characters? Why are the settings important to the story? Is there a contrast between some of the settings described so far?
- How does the way the characters in Chapter 4 express themselves differ? Do they use similar language? Do some express themselves more casually than others?
- What does the phrase 'raw cunning' mean in Chapter 3?
- What is a synonym for 'ancestral' in Chapter 4?
- What is a 'keekee'?

### Themes and conventions
- Consider Malicia's, Maurice's and Keith's attitudes to the truth. How do they differ? Is the author pointing out that Maurice's scheming and Malicia's fantasising lead to confusion, but Keith's reliance on truth will prevail?

**SESSION 3:** DANGER

## SESSION AIMS

Make sense of the text.

## BEFORE THE SESSION

The children should have read Chapter 4 prior to the session.

## READ

- Ask the children to talk to a partner about what has happened in the story so far and to scan Chapter 4 independently to remind themselves of recent events.

- Then involve the children in a brief group discussion. Ask them:
  - What is the girl's name?
  - Where does the girl take Maurice and Keith?
  - Why is Malicia shocked and horrified when Sardines appears?

- Ask the children: *What is strange about many of the things Malicia says? Does she concentrate on fact or fiction?* Then ask them to read Chapter 5 independently, keeping this type of detailed question in mind.

### During reading

- Ask the children to think about the information and the questions that arise for them as they read.

- If your school uses reading journals then the children should be encouraged to make notes as they read and consider each question.

- Move around the group and 'tune in' to hear individuals read aloud. Encourage and praise good expression.

## REVISIT AND RESPOND

Use the following discussion points to help the children think about what they have read in more depth.

**Note:** Since there are only 20 minutes for each session, you are advised to focus on only one or two of the elements that are listed below.

- Examine the effect of Malicia's presence on Maurice in Chapter 4. Ask the children: *Does Maurice talk or listen more? Does he feel the need to impress Malicia? Does she confuse him? What effect does Malicia have on Keith? Does he reveal more about himself?* Do the children think that Maurice and Keith become more interesting characters in the presence of Malicia?

- Use Chapter 4 to make a character study of Malicia. Ask: *What is odd about the things she says? How truthful is she? Why does she mention story situations so much?* Suggest that the children take turns being in the hot seat and, in role as Malicia, answering questions from the rest of the group. (You could use Activity 1 on page 32 of *Read and Respond The Amazing Maurice and His Educated Rodents* here.)

- Investigate the role that Darktan has, teaching and training other rats. What makes Darktan suitable for the role? What are his teaching methods? Is he successful? Encourage group discussion about the importance of Darktan to the rats.

- Direct the children to the point in Chapter 4 when Maurice decides that Malicia's mind 'worked in a different way to other people's minds'. Ask the children to re-read from there to the end of Chapter 4, searching for other suspicions by Maurice about Malicia's odd way of thinking and proof that he is correct. Bring the group together to share results.

- Examine the chapter headings for Chapters 4 and 5. Ask the children: *How are the text and appearance different from the rest of the chapter? What do the ragged edges tell the reader? Do the headers prepare us for what will happen in the chapter?* Debate the author's intentions. (You could use Activity 2 on page 38 of *Read and Respond The Amazing Maurice and His Educated Rodents* for help.)

- Work together on a character study of Darktan, using the information available by the end of Chapter 5. Enlist ideas from the children and make a list of characteristics on the whiteboard.

- Focus on the language used in Chapter 5 by re-reading the dialogue used by the rats. How does the author show differences in the rats' intelligence? Do some rats seem better thinkers than others? Does their speech reveal their personality? Encourage discussion as the children investigate.

Ask the children, whenever appropriate, to revisit the text to exemplify/support their answers.

Encourage the children to read aloud back to the group when referring back to the text – praise clear, confident and expressive reading.

## ASSESSMENT OPPORTUNITIES

The following bank of question prompts provides a quick and easy means of monitoring the children's comprehension skills and understanding of the text. The children's answers to a question must be supported by evidence from the text.

### Understanding

- Why does Darktan ask Nourishing to demonstrate how to make the trap safe?
- What has Darktan invented to help the Changelings recognise which tunnels are safe?
- Why does Malicia knock three times?
- How does Maurice decide to kill the mouse?
- What worries Darktan about the 'keekees' in this area?
- What does Darktan worry will start spreading among the Changelings?

### Inferences

- What does Darktan realise that the Changelings are facing in these tunnels?
- What would happen if the Changelings started behaving as ordinary rats?

- What do the Changelings mean by their 'invisible part'?
- Do the Changelings believe in the Bone Rat and the Big Rat Underground?
- Whose opinion on right and wrong do the Changelings seem to trust?

### Predictions

- What might happen in Chapter 6?

### Main ideas

- What is interesting about Maurice? Does the author make a clear distinction between this talking animal and the educated rats?
- Do the children think that Chapter 5 is an important point in the story? Why?

### Language, structure and presentation

- In Chapter 5, why does the author make frequent use of italic font in the rats' dialogue? Does it help the reader to learn more about the speaker?
- Consider the balance of dialogue and unspoken text in Chapters 4 and 5. Does the high proportion of dialogue move the plot along more quickly?
- What is an 'aiglet'?
- What is a 'guild'?

# SESSION 4: ADVENTURES

## SESSION AIMS

Discuss and explain the meaning of words in context.

## BEFORE THE SESSION

The children should have read Chapter 5 and the first five pages of Chapter 6 – up to 'I didn't expect this…' – prior to the session.

## READ

- Ask the children to talk to a partner about what has happened in the story so far and to scan Chapter 5 and the first five pages of Chapter 6 independently to remind themselves of recent events.
- Then involve the children in a brief group discussion. Ask them:
  - Why does Malicia insist on them using a secret knock?
  - What is ridiculous about Malicia's attempts not to be noticed by people?
  - Will Malicia be shocked if she hears Maurice's swear word?
- Ask the children: *What does Maurice mean when he says 'I don't do clothes'?* Then ask them to read the rest of Chapter 6 independently, keeping this question in mind.

### During reading

- Ask the children to think about the information and the questions that arise for them as they read.
- If your school uses reading journals then the children should be encouraged to make notes as they read and consider each question.
- Move around the group and 'tune in' to hear individuals read aloud. Encourage and praise good expression.

## REVISIT AND RESPOND

Use the following discussion points to help the children think about what they have read in more depth.

**Note:** Since there are only 20 minutes for each session, you are advised to focus on only one or two of the elements that are listed below.

- Investigate the dialogue between Maurice and Malicia in the first few pages of Chapter 6. How many times is Maurice surprised by what Malicia says or does? How often are they annoyed by each other? How does their annoyance show in their language? Encourage discussion as the group shares examples.
- Explore the reaction of the listening Keith to Malicia's explanation of her use of a hairpin, as in the fairy story *The Seventh Wife of Greenbeard*. Does Keith believe her? Ask the children to put themselves in Keith's place. Would they believe Malicia when she says it is one of the 'Grim Fairy-Tales'? Why?
- Consider the name Malicia. Ask the children: *Do you find the name strange? Does it remind you of another word?* Then ask: *What does 'malice' mean?* Encourage the group to exchange views about the author's intention in his choice of name. Is he making fun of his character or revealing her personality?
- Debate the wisdom of Dangerous Beans's behaviour. Should he treat the living keekee as a friend or an enemy? Is Dangerous Beans foolish to let the living keekee go? Why does he treat her as an equal? Encourage the children to listen to one another's views before reaching a majority decision.
- Point out the thoughts of Peaches as Darktan and Hamnpork disagree: 'This is the showdown. This is where we find out who is leader.' Do the children agree with Peaches? Is Hamnpork safe in his position as leader?
- Examine Hamnpork's state of mind. Ask the children: *Is he happy being a Changeling? Is he sure of how he should behave? Which of his words and*

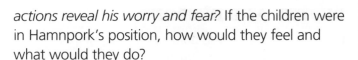

*actions reveal his worry and fear?* If the children were in Hamnpork's position, how would they feel and what would they do?

Ask the children, whenever appropriate, to revisit the text to exemplify/support their answers.

Encourage the children to read aloud back to the group when referring back to the text – praise clear, confident and expressive reading.

## ASSESSMENT OPPORTUNITIES

The following bank of question prompts provides a quick and easy means of monitoring the children's comprehension skills and understanding of the text. The children's answers to a question must be supported by evidence from the text.

### Understanding

- How many knocks are in Malicia's secret knock?
- What does Maurice refuse to do?
- What is on the sign hanging over the door to a black building?
- How does Malicia open the padlock?
- Which of his senses does Hamnpork rely on?
- Why does Malicia keep leaning against the wall of the shed?

### Inferences

- Why does Maurice look at Keith for help when Malicia talks about a secret switch?
- Why does Malicia say, 'Some people totally fail to have any idea of how to design a proper secret passage'?
- Does Malicia take the situation seriously? Is she enjoying what is happening?
- Why does Hamnpork not like the idea of baths?
- Who is Mr Clicky?

### Predicting

- What might happen in Chapter 7?

### Main ideas

- Is the original plan getting out of Maurice's control? Are he, Keith and the Changelings trapped in Bad Blintz? What words or happenings in Chapter 6 make you think this?
- Consider the greater detail about the Changelings in this part of the book. Are they becoming more interesting characters? Is the author emphasising the differences between them?

### Language, structure and presentation

- Consider the use of italic font for some words in Chapter 4. Why do you think the author uses this device? What does it tell the reader?
- What does the word 'nonchalance' mean?
- What is the 'grapnel' that Malicia has in her bag? What is it for?
- Why does the author use the words 'clonk' and 'gloink' to describe some sounds? Do you find them effective?

# SESSION 5: FEAR

## SESSION AIMS

Read books that are structured in different ways.

## BEFORE THE SESSION

The children should have read Chapter 6 and the first six pages of Chapter 7 – up to 'Boss', said Sardines, 'this is serious!' – prior to the session.

## READ

- Ask the children to talk to a partner about what has happened in the story so far and to scan Chapter 6 and the first six pages of Chapter 7 (as far as 'Boss', said Sardines, 'this is serious!') independently, to remind themselves of recent events.

- Then involve the children in a brief group discussion. Ask them:
  - What room are Maurice, Malicia and Keith in?
  - What is the cellar filled with?
  - Who does Maurice mistakenly attack?

- Ask the children: *What do you notice about the paragraph division after 'Boss', said Sardines, 'this is serious!'?* Then ask them to read the rest of Chapter 7 independently, keeping this question in mind.

### During reading

- Ask the children to think about the information and the questions that arise for them as they read.

- If your school uses reading journals then the children should be encouraged to make notes as they read and consider each question.

- Move around the group and 'tune in' to hear individuals read aloud. Encourage and praise good expression.

## REVISIT AND RESPOND

Use the following discussion points to help the children think about what they have read in more depth.

**Note:** Since there are only 20 minutes for each session, you are advised to only focus on one or two of the elements that are listed below.

- Examine Malicia's reaction to the trapdoor and point out her reference to 'an adventure'. Does she realise that the situation is serious? Does she think she is involved in a storytelling game? Share views and evidence.

- Investigate the structure of the book so far. Ask the children: *Is it written in the first or third person? How is the text organised? Are chapters the most appropriate length? Are there frequent changes of setting? If you were the author, would you organise the story differently?* (At this point you could use ideas from Activity 5 on page 25 of *Read and Respond The Amazing Maurice and His Educated Rodents*.)

- Consider the dialogue between Maurice and Malicia in Chapter 7. Do they speak politely to each other? Do they understand each other? What is Maurice's verbal weapon? Share examples of confusion, wit and sarcasm. Which of the two characters do the children sympathise with? Ask them: *Is that what the author most likely wants? Why do you think this?*

- Study the character development of Maurice. What detective skills does he demonstrate near the beginning of Chapter 7? As the children identify examples, write them on the whiteboard. Ask: *What does the reader learn about Maurice? Is more information given later when Maurice thinks about his own safety and seeks escape?*

- Discuss the character of Keith. Ask: *How has the author presented Keith from the start of the book? Does he become a more interesting character in Chapter 7? How?* Are the children surprised, in the early pages of Chapter 7, by Keith's comment about wire netting? What does this show about Keith?

- Direct the children to the description of the caged rats to re-read. Which senses are appealed to? As the children quote text, write it on the whiteboard. Are the words effective? What descriptions would the children add?

- Examine the emotional struggles of Hamnpork. What internal conflict does he feel? Does he stay a Changeling? Do old instincts overcome his educated thinking? Encourage discussion about Hamnpork's thoughts and behaviour.

Ask the children, whenever appropriate, to revisit the text to exemplify/support their answers.

Encourage them to read aloud back to the group when referring back to the text – praise clear, confident and expressive reading.

## ASSESSMENT OPPORTUNITIES

The following bank of question prompts provides a quick and easy means of monitoring the children's comprehension skills and understanding of the text. The children's answers to a question must be supported by evidence from the text.

### Understanding
- Why is it shocking that there is so much food in the cellar?
- Who brings a storybook along?
- Why does Dangerous Beans start crying?
- Which rats are in cages?
- Why is Hamnpork trembling with rage?
- Who bites Keith?

### Inferences
- Why has Peaches brought the book *Mr Bunnsy Has an Adventure*?
- Why does Keith put Hamnpork down on the floor 'very carefully' after Hamnpork bites him?
- Why do some of the Changelings forget how to talk?
- Who is talking to Maurice in the final pages of Chapter 7?
- Which unknown rats does Maurice smell?

### Predicting
- What might happen in Chapter 8?

### Main ideas
- How does the author add a serious and thought-provoking tone to a story that is often funny? Why could the reader worry about the fate of some of the characters?
- Why does the author use speaking animals as some of his characters? Is the author expressing serious human views through these characters?

### Language, structure and presentation
- How did the author decide where to end sections of Chapter 7? Is the chapter divided at appropriate times? Are the divisions obvious? Would you change the structure?
- What does 'gnaw' mean?
- Why does Keith use 'us' when he shouts at Malicia not to attack Hamnpork?

# SESSION 6: EMOTIONS

## SESSION AIMS

Consider character attitudes, feelings and thoughts and reader response.

## BEFORE THE SESSION

The children should have read half of Chapter 8 (up to 'We'd better see what's happened to the kid,' he said') prior to the session.

## READ

- Ask the children to talk to a partner about what has happened in the story so far and to scan the first half of Chapter 8 (up to 'We'd better see what's happened to the kid,' he said') independently, to remind themselves of recent events.
- Then involve the children in a brief group discussion. Ask them:
  - How is Maurice reunited with the Changelings?
  - How does Dangerous Beans react to seeing Maurice? How does Darktan's response differ?
  - What has happened to Hamnpork?
- Ask the children: *Are you surprised that Maurice is unhappy about eating Additives?* Then ask them to read the rest of Chapter 8, keeping this type of question in mind.

### During reading

- Ask the children to think about the information and the questions that arise for them as they read.
- If your school uses reading journals then the children should be encouraged to make notes as they read and consider each question.
- Move around the group and 'tune in' to hear individuals read aloud. Encourage and praise good expression.

## REVISIT AND RESPOND

Use the following discussion points to help the children think about what they have read in more depth.

**Note:** Since there are only 20 minutes for each session, you are advised to focus on only one or two of the elements that are listed below.

- New aspects of Maurice's character are evident in Chapter 8. Ask the children which aspects of his character they find surprising or particularly interesting. What does he do or say to reveal the character traits? The children should refer to the text to support their views.
- Compare the atmosphere and mood of Chapter 8 with that of Chapter 7. Ask the children: *How does the atmosphere and mood differ between chapters? What effect does Chapter 8 have on your attitude to Maurice and his feelings about the Changelings?*
- Encourage the children to think about how they would feel if they were Maurice being questioned about Additives. What would they say? Would they admit to eating him? You could use a conscience alley situation to explore what Maurice decides to say (see also Activity 6 on page 34 of *Read and Respond The Amazing Maurice and His Educated Rodents*).
- Examine the conversation between Malicia and Keith. Ask the children: *How does Keith feel about the Changelings? Who criticises the Changelings' names? Who defends them? Which of the two speakers do the children agree with?*
- Ask the children to work as a group to investigate the rescue of Hamnpork. Suggest creating a timeline of the actions involved. Is the rescue a complete success? Do the children think Hamnpork's position as leader is strengthened or weakened now?

- Ask the children to re-read the final pages of Chapter 8. Discuss Darktan's actions. Ask them: *What qualities does he show as he fights Jacko? How does he escape from Jacko? Why is the final line of the chapter a shock? Is this what the author intends?*

- Consider how authors can reveal character personalities. Share ideas and list the methods authors use. Does the author sometimes let readers decide for themselves? Refer the children to where Maurice and the rats meet up, early in Chapter 8. Point out that Darktan gives Maurice 'a much more knowing look' and says: 'Depend on him to do what, though?' What can the reader infer about Darktan, Dangerous Beans and Maurice? Let the children consider what else they can work out about characters from events in this chapter. (At this point you could use Activity 4 on page 26 of *Read and Respond The Amazing Maurice and His Educated Rodents*.)

Ask the children, whenever appropriate, to revisit the text to exemplify/support their answers.

Encourage the children to read aloud back to the group when referring back to the text – praise clear, confident and expressive reading.

## ASSESSMENT OPPORTUNITIES

The following bank of question prompts provides a quick and easy means of monitoring the children's comprehension skills and understanding of the text. The children's answers to a question must be supported by evidence from the text.

### Understanding
- Why does Darktan want to rescue Hamnpork?
- What happens to Nourishing to make her 'wet and dejected'?
- Who was the rat with a stammer?
- Why does Peaches read aloud from *Mr Bunnsy Has an Adventure*?

- What is emptied into the pit first?
- What is dropped into the pit afterwards?

### Inferences
- What is Darktan's length of wood with a red blob on the end?
- What does Darktan want Nourishing to do when he says 'I want them to remember tonight?'
- Why are men crowded round the pit?
- Why does Hamnpork scream 'Idiots!'?
- Why does Darktan dive into a dark place that he cannot check first?

### Predicting
- What might happen in Chapter 9? Will Darktan be safe?

### Main ideas
- What new storyline is introduced into the plot in Chapter 8? Does it make the story more sinister?
- Why does the author give Peaches a larger role and more dialogue in Chapter 8? What effect does this have on the reader's attitude to her and her importance to the Changelings and their plans?

### Language, structure and presentation
- How does the author build up atmosphere and information about the characters in Chapter 8?
- What is a 'stammer'?
- How does Malicia's attitude to the Changelings begin to change during Chapter 8? Does she start to care about them?
- Why does the author use italic font for a long paragraph in the middle of Chapter 8? What is the effect on the reader?

**SESSION 7:** UNCERTAINTY

## SESSION AIMS

Ask questions to improve understanding of the text.

## BEFORE THE SESSION

The children should have read half of Chapter 10 – up to 'And so, in your despair, you come at last to me' – prior to the session.

## READ

- Ask the children to talk to a partner about what has happened in the story so far and to scan the first half of Chapter 10 (as far as 'And so, in your despair, you come at last to me') independently or with a partner, to remind themselves of recent events.
- Then involve the children in a brief group discussion. Ask them:
  - What is Maurice's plan for his own future?
  - Why does Sardines not take Hamnpork along the washing lines?
  - Why does Darktan nod to Sardines to snuff out the candle?
- Ask the children: *How does Darktan decide how to behave at the death of Hamnpork?* (This question focuses on story information that the reader is left wanting to ask questions about.) Then ask them to read the rest of Chapter 10 independently, keeping this type of question in mind.

### During reading

- Ask the children to think about the information and the questions that arise for them as they read.
- If your school uses reading journals then the children should be encouraged to make notes as they read and consider each question.
- Move around the group and 'tune in' to hear individuals read aloud. Encourage and praise good expression.

## REVISIT AND RESPOND

Use the following discussion points to help the children think about what they have read in more depth.

**Note:** Since there are only 20 minutes for each session, you are advised to focus on only one or two of the elements that are listed below.

- Ask the children to find examples of important questions that Darktan is asked after the old leader, Hamnpork, dies. Encourage the children to put themselves in a Changeling's place: your leader has just died; Darktan seems to be taking charge; what questions would you ask Darktan?
- Examine Darktan's relationship with Sardines. How do the two Changelings feel about each other? Do they treat each other as equals? How does Darktan show his leadership qualities? How is Sardines a help to him?
- Examine the changes that take place in Darktan during Chapter 10. Ask the children: *Is it significant that Darktan wonders about the Big Rat? Does it mean that he is close to death?* Point out the opinion that, after his rescue, Darktan was different: 'his thoughts had slowed down, but got bigger'. *Is he more appreciative of the intelligent words and thoughts of Dangerous Beans? Why? What dangers does Darktan now recognise?* Debate whether Darktan has become wiser.
- Direct the children to Hamnpork's death scene. Point out that Hamnpork whispers to Darktan just before he dies. Ask the children to put themselves in Hamnpork's place. What essential message or advice would they want to pass on?
- Investigate the changes and struggles in Dangerous Beans in Chapter 10. Examine the debate between Peaches and Dangerous Beans. Why does Dangerous Beans change his attitude to *Mr Bunnsy* and the Rules? Point out how Dangerous Beans struggles to stay free of the Spider's enticing voice. Ask the children: *What do the words 'I am more than just a rat' tell you about Dangerous Beans?*

- Consider the importance that the two minor characters, Sardines and Peaches, have in Chapter 10. Why are they important? What is their role? What do they achieve? Share ideas. Can the group decide who is more important? Remind the children to support their ideas with evidence from the text.

- Suggest that the author often provokes questions in the reader's mind. Guide the children through scanning Chapter 9. Ask: *What questions are in your mind by the end of the chapter?* Share some ideas. Write one question on the whiteboard that is answered in Chapter 10; for example: *Will Hamnpork recover?* Allow the children to scan Chapter 10 together. Encourage discussion about questions they want answered by the chapter's end. (At this point you could use Activity 8 on page 28 of *Read and Respond The Amazing Maurice and His Educated Rodents.*)

Ask the children, whenever appropriate, to revisit the text to exemplify/support their answers.

Encourage the children to read aloud back to the group when referring back to the text – praise clear, confident and expressive reading.

## ASSESSMENT OPPORTUNITIES

The following bank of question prompts provides a quick and easy means of monitoring the children's comprehension skills and understanding of the text. The children's answers to a question must be supported by evidence from the text.

### Understanding

- Why is it dark in the cellar when Hamnpork dies?
- Who has to act as leader?
- Do the Changelings eat the dead Hamnpork?
- What will mark Hamnpork's grave?
- Does Malicia really believe in rat kings?
- Who drops *Mr Bunnsy*? Who says he no longer cares?

### Inferences

- How does Sardines persuade Darktan to act as a strong leader?
- What is fitting about the two ways in which Hamnpork's grave is to be marked?
- How does Darktan feel about leadership?
- Why does Darktan not reveal what Hamnpork said to him as he died?
- Why do the other Changelings respect and obey Darktan?

### Predicting

- What might happen in Chapter 11?

### Main ideas

- Why are the rat-catchers not involved in Chapter 10? Does the author still have to join all the threads of the story together? Does this chapter leave the reader with many questions unanswered?

### Language, structure and presentation

- Why did the author make Chapter 10 so long? Could it have been divided at exciting points? Does Chapter 10 end at an interesting time?
- Why is it a 'ragged cheer' from the Clan? What does the expression mean?
- What is a synonym for 'beguiling' towards the end of Chapter 10?
- What distinction does Dangerous Beans see between 'a rat' and 'vermin'?

### Themes and conventions

- How does the author create an air of mystery and menace around the Spider and the Big Rat? Do the children feel that new, more serious themes are added to the story in this chapter?

# ▼ SESSION 8: COMPROMISES

## SESSION AIMS

Identify themes and conventions.

## BEFORE THE SESSION

The children should have read half of Chapter 12 – up to 'Perhaps it's a map' – prior to the session.

## READ

- Ask the children to talk to a partner about what has happened in the story so far and to scan half of Chapter 12 (as far as 'Perhaps it's a map') independently, to remind themselves of recent events.

- Then involve the children in a brief group discussion. Ask them:
  - Who negotiates between the humans and the rats?
  - Why will the town clock attract tourists?
  - What does Dangerous Beans now believe about *Mr Bunnsy Has an Adventure*?

- Ask the children: *Why does Dangerous Beans agree to stop looking for an island?* (This question focuses on the future dreams of the characters and their willingness to compromise.) Then ask the children to read the rest of Chapter 12 independently, keeping this type of question in mind.

### During reading

- Ask the children to think about the information and the questions that arise for them as they read.

- If your school uses reading journals then the children should be encouraged to make notes as they read and consider each question.

- Move around the group and 'tune in' to hear individuals read aloud. Encourage and praise good expression.

## REVISIT AND RESPOND

Use the following discussion points to help the children think about what they have read in more depth.

**Note:** Since there are only 20 minutes for each session, you are advised to focus on only one or two of the elements that are listed below.

- Investigate the effect of Darktan's answer in Chapter 12 as Dangerous Beans talks of his original hope of an island. What persuades Dangerous Beans to accept Bad Blintz as a place to stay? Do the children think he will be happy?

- Assess Maurice's skill as he tries to make peace between rats and humans. What are Maurice's strengths? What are his weaknesses? If the children were Maurice, what other action would they take to negotiate an agreement between the rats and the humans? Share ideas.

- Examine Darktan and the mayor's conversation. Ask the children: *What does each learn from the other? What does Darktan feel about being a leader? What does he decide about the new arrangement of living together?* The children could use a hot-seat activity to role play Darktan and express his thoughts (see, for example, Activity 1 on page 32 of *Read and Respond The Amazing Maurice and His Educated Rodents*).

- Question why Maurice rejects a comfortable life in Bad Blintz. What does Maurice do? How does he show generosity? Are the children surprised by Maurice's behaviour at this point?

- Discuss the events of Chapter 12. Encourage the children to consider the chapter in relation to the whole book. Are there plot questions from earlier in the book that the author has still not answered? Ask the group to compile a list.

- Question the children about the function of Chapter 12. Does the chapter satisfy the

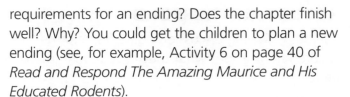

requirements for an ending? Does the chapter finish well? Why? You could get the children to plan a new ending (see, for example, Activity 6 on page 40 of *Read and Respond The Amazing Maurice and His Educated Rodents*).

- Point out that Chapter 12 has a change of setting, focus and atmosphere from previous chapters, with the characters inside places such as the Rathaus's council hall or the mayor's private office. Point out examples of rats and humans speaking to each other as equals. Do the animals and humans all want the unusual project to be a success? How is this an example to other towns?

- Discuss the structure of this book. How is it divided? Do the children think the author could have organised the book in a different way? Share ideas. Which of the proposed structures is the most popular?

- Suggest that an author could decide to write a sequel to this story. Share predictions about what might happen in the new book.

Ask the children, whenever appropriate, to revisit the text to exemplify/support their answers.

Encourage the children to read aloud back to the group when referring back to the text – praise clear, confident and expressive reading.

## ASSESSMENT OPPORTUNITIES

The following bank of question prompts provides a quick and easy means of monitoring the children's comprehension skills and understanding of the text. The children's answers to a question must be supported by evidence from the text.

### Understanding
- What is found in a wooden box under a floorboard?
- Why does Maurice make himself the negotiator?
- Who will be the town's rat piper?
- What else does Keith aim to become?

- Who gives Darktan 'a long, thoughtful stare' during the meeting?
- Which rat frightens some of the councillors?

### Inferences
- Why is Keith impressed that Malicia's expression does not change when he explains how rats mark their tunnels?
- What does Malicia mean when she talks about making 'important mental adjustments'?
- Why will rat-catchers no longer be needed in Bad Blintz?
- Why will the woodcarvers in the town become richer?

### Predicting
- How will Malicia and Keith get on in future?
- Consider what has happened to the main characters. Will they be happy and successful?

### Main ideas
- Is Maurice happier at the end of the story or at the beginning? Why? Do you think he will keep thinking about his time in Bad Blintz? Why?
- Consider what has happened to the main characters. Have they made wise decisions?

### Language, structure and presentation
- List details that the author mentions in Chapter 12 to emphasise the confusion sometimes felt by animals or people about the new arrangement.
- What are 'ill-gotten gains'?
- What is a synonym for 'tatty'?

### Themes and conventions
- Consider examples in Chapter 12 of rats and humans speaking to each other as equals. Is the author emphasising the need for people to show mutual respect in order to live together peacefully?

# SESSION 1: EARLY DAYS

## SESSION AIMS

Meet and begin to learn about the two key characters of Joey and Albert.
Identify how language choice contributes to pace and character.

## READ

- Ask the children what the cover suggests the book is about. (If they are familiar with the film or stage production, ask them to bear this in mind as they read the book, comparing the different versions.)

- Ask the children to read silently the Author's Note. Do they know the significance of the date – 1914? Ask: *What does this suggest to you?* They may guess that the story is based on fact – something they can check later online.

- Ask: *How does the author show us where he got his idea from for the story? Why does he think it's an important story to tell?*

- Ask the children to read the first two paragraphs of Chapter 1, noticing that it is written in the first person; in the voice of a horse. Ask: *Why do you think Michael Morpurgo has chosen to write the story in this way?* For example, we will be seeing his life and adventures from the central character's own viewpoint.

### During reading

- Ask the children to read independently to the end of the chapter. As they read ask them to compare the characters of the horse's new owner and his son (Albert's dad and Albert). Ask them to be aware of how descriptive language is used.

- If your school uses reading journals then the children should be encouraged to make notes as they read and consider each question.

- Move around the group and 'tune in' to hear individuals read aloud. Encourage and praise good expression.

## REVISIT AND RESPOND

Use the following discussion points to help the children think about what they have read in more depth.

**Note:** Since there are only 20 minutes for each session, you are advised to focus on only one or two of the elements that are listed below.

- Ask the children if they think Joey and his mother realised what was happening when they were taken to the horse sale. How do we know that Joey missed his mother and that she wanted to get back to him? Do they think that horses have feelings, the same as humans? Ask for their reasons.

- Ask: *What did Joey see as the difference between his 'owner' and his 'master'?* Do the children agree with this distinction?

- Invite the children to identify words in paragraphs 3 and 4 that show how the men treated Joey after he was sold. For example: 'harsh', 'lunge', 'screamed', 'bolted', 'charging', 'stranded', 'violently', 'tightening', 'dragged', 'wrenched', 'exhaustion', 'vicious', and so on.

- Ask the children to identify words and phrases at the end of the chapter, from 'Albert was about the same height as me', that show how Albert treated Joey; for example: 'calmed', 'smoothed', 'gently', 'dabbed', 'sweet hay', 'smiled broadly', 'stroked', 'don't worry', 'understand', 'bind', 'trust', 'affection'. Compare these words with those of the men earlier in the chapter. Discuss how the vocabulary choice tells us about the characters and how it affects the pace of the narrative.

- Invite the children to express their opinions about the characters of Albert and his father, giving their reasons.

Ask the children, whenever appropriate, to revisit the text to exemplify/support their answers.

Encourage the children to read aloud back to the group when referring back to the text – praise clear, confident and expressive reading.

## Before the next session

Ask the children to read Chapters 2 and 3, noting the ways in which Albert trains Joey and the deepening bond between them.

## ASSESSMENT OPPORTUNITIES

The following bank of question prompts provides a quick and easy means of monitoring the children's comprehension skills and understanding of the text. The children's answers to a question must be supported by evidence from the text.

### Understanding

- How old was Joey when he was sold?
- What job did Joey's mother do?
- Why did Joey think he was difficult to sell?
- Why did Joey back away from the men when he was put in the pen after the sale?
- Where was Joey taken to live after he had been sold?
- What reason is given for Albert's dad being badly behaved on market days?
- What does Albert plan to do with Joey 'when he's ready'?
- How old is Albert at the start of the story?
- What reason did Albert's mother give for his dad buying the horse? What did he actually go for?
- What did Albert do to calm and welcome Joey?
- How did Joey show Albert that he was thanking him?
- Why did Albert call the horse Joey?

### Inferences

- How does the men's treatment of Joey when he was in the pen show us what they are like?
- How did Joey feel when he first arrived at his new home? Why do you say that?
- Who did Joey's new owner call an 'old ratbag'? What does this tell us about his attitude to his animals?
- How can we tell, from his first words to his mother about Joey, that Albert is different from his father?
- How do we know Albert was pleased that his dad bought the horse?

- What does Albert think about his father's relationship with horses?
- How does Joey know that he has 'found a friend for life' in Albert?
- What can you tell about Zoey from the final sentence?

### Predicting

- What do you think will happen next to Joey and Albert?

### Main ideas

- Do you agree with Albert's mother and father that horses don't understand when people talk to them, and that they are 'obstinate and stupid'? Give reasons for your answer. What do you think the author's feelings are about this? How can you tell?

### Language, structure and presentation

- What does 'nickered' mean? Can you work out its meaning from the context?
- Explain why you think the story is written in the voice of the horse, Joey.

### Themes and conventions

- If you had not read the title of the book, what would you say was the theme of the story, based on what you have read so far?

# SESSION 2: CHANGES

## SESSION AIMS

Identify how the author evokes emotion. Consider key characters' reactions to the developing situation in the story, in relation to the war and how it is beginning to affect them.

## BEFORE THE SESSION

The children should have read Chapters 2 and 3 prior to the session.

## READ

- Ask the children to reflect on the events of Chapters 2 and 3. Invite them to share their thoughts about how Albert trained Joey in various ways, and how this deepened the bond between them. Ask: *Is this what Joey meant when he said he had only one master?*

- Why do the children think it was so important that Albert trained Joey to pull a plough? How did his attitude towards Joey change during this training, and why? Do they think Joey realised what was happening? We are led to believe that Joey understands human speech and body language: is this accurate, or is it just being used as a way of telling the story?

- How did Albert's parents react when war was declared? Why might they have felt differently about it?

- Invite the children to discuss Albert's attitude towards his father. Was his mother justified in what she offered as an explanation for the way her husband behaved?

- What made Joey suspicious about Albert's father's behaviour at the end of Chapter 3?

- Invite the children to predict what will happen next, based on the ending of Chapter 3.

### During reading

- Ask the children to read Chapter 4 during this session. As they read, ask them to think about the feelings and emotions the chapter invokes.

- If your school uses reading journals then the children should be encouraged to make notes as they read and consider each question.

- Move around the group and 'tune in' to hear individuals read aloud. Encourage and praise good expression.

## REVISIT AND RESPOND

Use the following discussion points to help the children think about what they have read in more depth.

**Note:** Since there are only 20 minutes for each session, you are advised to focus on only one or two of the elements that are listed below.

- Ask the children if they suspected that Joey would have to be taken away to be part of the war. What made them think this, or was it a complete surprise to them? Do they think Albert had expected this outcome? Ask them to give reasons for their answer.

- Invite the children to find examples in the text that demonstrate the atmosphere in the village when Albert's father arrives with the horses. Can they find a section later in the chapter, when Albert arrives, that shows how the atmosphere changes?

- Ask the children to share their observations on the emotions and feelings that are shown for Joey, Albert, Albert's father and Captain Nicholls.

- How did the children feel, reading this chapter? What was it about the writing that made them feel that way?

- Ask the children to explain why the author described Albert's father as 'a shrunken man'.

- Invite the children's predictions for what might happen next in the story. Do they think Joey will ever be reunited with Albert?

Ask the children, whenever appropriate, to revisit the text to exemplify/support their answers.

Encourage the children to read aloud back to the group when referring back to the text – praise clear, confident and expressive reading.

## Before the next session

Ask the children to read Chapters 5 and 6 in preparation for the next session. Ask them to make notes about the new characters that come into Joey's life, and how he feels towards them.

## ASSESSMENT OPPORTUNITIES

The following bank of question prompts provides a quick and easy means of monitoring the children's comprehension skills and understanding of the text. The children's answers to a question must be supported by evidence from the text.

### Understanding

- What was unusual and suspicious about Albert's father's manner and behaviour at the start of the chapter?
- What is Captain Nicholls' opinion of Joey?
- Why was Joey not feeling frightened when the army vets took him to be examined?
- What was the vet's opinion of Joey?
- How much was Joey sold for?
- What did Albert's father do that made Joey see him as 'almost a likeable man'? Does this change your opinion of him?
- What did Joey do when he realised that he 'was being abandoned'? What was Zoey's reaction?
- What was the minimum age for a soldier?
- Why did Albert want to join the army?
- Why could Albert not join the army?

### Inferences

- How do we know that Joey and Zoey didn't know where they were going when Albert's father led them out of the stable?
- Why was Joey both excited and apprehensive as they approached the village?
- What was the mood of the villagers when Albert and the horses arrived? How do you know?
- How do we know that Albert's father had arranged to sell the horses before he came into the village that morning?

- Why do you think the army was looking to buy horses?
- Do you think Albert would believe Captain Nicholls' promise to take care of Joey? Why do you think that? Would you believe him? Why/why not?

### Predicting

- What do you think might happen to Joey and to Albert next in the story?
- What do you think Albert would say to his father when they get home? What would Albert's mother have to say?

### Main ideas

- How do you think Albert felt when he realised his father had sold Joey?
- How would Joey and Albert feel when they parted? What might each of them be thinking and hoping?
- Consider the character of Albert's father. How have we seen him apparently change since the beginning of the book? Explain why you think this is.

### Language, structure and presentation

- Use a dictionary to find the meaning of the words 'khaki', 'jodhpurs', 'fetlocks'.

# SESSION 3: OFF TO WAR

## SESSION AIMS

Consider the way in which humans relate to Joey and how he reacts to them.
Identify effective descriptive writing.

## READ

- Ask the children to list the new characters Joey meets in Chapter 5 and 6, briefly describing his relationship with each one.

- Ask: *What new experiences did Joey have after being bought by the army? How did he feel about them?* For example, he found army training hard, despite being used to hard work on the farm; he disliked his rider Corporal Simon Perkins.

- Invite the children to describe the difference Captain Nicholls made to Joey's time in training.

- Have the children noticed the way people talk at length to Joey? What do they talk to him about? Why do the children think they do this?

- Have the children noticed the link between the painting in the author's note and Captain Nicholls' painting of Joey?

- Invite the children to compare the characters of Captain Nicholls and Corporal Perkins.

- In what ways do we see Topthorn and Joey becoming close?

- Invite the children to describe the new sights and sounds that Joey encountered after arriving in France.

- Ask the children their opinions about the description of the battle, and their feelings about the sudden death of Captain Nicholls.

- Invite the children to predict what will happen next.

### Before reading

- Ask the children to read Chapter 7 in the next part of this session. As they read, ask them to identify sections of the writing they find particularly effective in describing events or showing characters' feelings.

- If your school uses reading journals then the children should be encouraged to make notes as they read and consider each question.

- Move around the group and 'tune in' to hear individuals read aloud. Encourage and praise good expression.

## REVISIT AND RESPOND

Use the following discussion points to help the children think about what they have read in more depth.

**Note:** Since there are only 20 minutes for each session, you are advised to focus on only one or two of the elements that are listed below.

- Invite the children to consider the relationships Joey has with Captain Stewart and Trooper Warren. In what ways are they similar and in what ways do they differ?

- In Chapter 7 yet another character talks at length to Joey – Trooper Warren. He even reads his letter from home to the horse. Invite the children to suggest why this device has been included. For example, it allows us as readers to discover more about the characters talking to Joey and is a way of showing us the wider aspects of the war that Joey is not experiencing.

- What do the children think about the contents of Trooper Warren's letter? What would Trooper Warren have thought about them? The letter is quite short and has very little information in it; it doesn't mention the war or ask questions. Why might this be? They may suggest that such a letter would be comforting for the Trooper as it describes normal home life, taking him away momentarily from the war and giving him something to look forward to when he – hopefully – returns home.

- Invite the children to share a section of the text they have chosen that they feel is particularly well written in terms of description or evoking feelings or emotions, explaining the reasons for their choice.

Ask the children, whenever appropriate, to revisit the text to exemplify/support their answers.

Encourage the children to read aloud back to the group when referring back to the text – praise clear, confident and expressive reading

## Before the next session

Ask the children to read Chapters 8 and 9 in preparation for the next session, noting Joey's new experiences and how he deals with them.

## ASSESSMENT OPPORTUNITIES

The following bank of question prompts provides a quick and easy means of monitoring the children's comprehension skills and understanding of the text. The children's answers to a question must be supported by evidence from the text.

### Understanding

- What role did Captain Stewart take on for Joey after Captain Nicholls' death?
- What did Captain Stewart ask Joey to do for Trooper Warren?
- Why did Trooper Warren seem nervous when he met Joey? What do we learn later that would have made him particularly nervous?
- Why did Joey no longer walk beside Topthorn when the squadron went out?
- How did Joey know that Trooper Warren wasn't used to riding horses?
- How did Trooper Warren treat Joey?
- How did Joey's role change that first autumn of the war?
- What was Trooper Warren's job before he joined the army?
- What difference had Joey made to Trooper Warren?
- What differences did the heavy rain make to the men and horses?
- In what ways did Trooper Warren take good care of Joey during the winter?
- What was different between the soldiers going to and returning from battle?

### Inferences

- What is implied by 'there were always two or three horses without riders'?
- Do you think other horses are talked to in the same way as Joey? Give reasons for your answer.
- Why had Trooper Warren thought he wouldn't ride a horse again after his first battle?

- How did Joey get to know what was happening in the war?
- Why did the cavalry need the muddy ground to harden?
- How do we know that Joey's squadron was near to the fighting?

### Predicting

- What do you think will happen next for Joey?

### Main ideas

- In what ways has Joey's life changed since he arrived in France?

### Language, structure and presentation

- What does 'skirmishes' mean? Can you work out the meaning from the context in which it is used?
- What is the difference between cavalry and infantry?
- Skim the chapter, making a list of words that are to do with the army and the fighting.

### Themes and conventions

- Explain how the one-sided conversations that people have with Joey helps the story to move forward. How does it help us as readers?

# SESSION 4: CAPTURED

## SESSION AIMS

Identify how the author shows us the effects of war on all participants.
Consider the effect the presence of the two horses has on the humans they encounter.

## READ

- Ask the children what they noticed about the atmosphere and pace of the opening of Chapter 8, leading up to the battle. (It is calm and quiet then builds to a vivid crescendo as the battle ensues.) Did they also notice that the calm and quiet return at the end of the chapter? Ask them how this contrast makes the vivid description of the battle even stronger. How did reading this make the children feel?

- Invite the children to describe the character of Herr Hauptmann, referring to examples in the text. Ask them to describe how he feels about Joey, and how he treats him.

- Chapters 8 and 9 show us something of the war from the German perspective. Invite the children to explain what they think Michael Morpurgo's purpose might have been by including both perspectives. Ask them: *Does Morpurgo intend to show us that war is the same for both sides? What similarities and differences can you see between the British and German experiences?*

- Explore what might happen in the following chapter. Who might the girl and her grandfather be, and what part might they play in how the story unfolds?

- Overall, what effect do the children think Joey's experiences so far would have on him?

### During reading

- Ask the children to think about the information and the questions that arise for them as they read Chapter 10.

- If your school uses reading journals then the children should be encouraged to make notes as they read and consider each question.

- Move around the group and 'tune in' to hear individuals read aloud. Encourage and praise good expression.

## REVISIT AND RESPOND

Use the following discussion points to help the children think about what they have read in more depth.

**Note:** Since there are only 20 minutes for each session, you are advised to focus on only one or two of the elements that are listed below.

- Joey and Topthorn spend the next months working at the German field hospital. Invite the children to identify how we know their presence made a difference to the soldiers; for example, the children could refer to the obvious pleasure of the soldiers when the horses were cheered as they passed them on the road; when the injured soldier gave Joey his Iron Cross medal, and the treats they brought to them; the job the horses did was appreciated.

- Ask the children to reflect on the various people who have so far taken care of Joey, compared to the experiences he has had. Do they think Joey is lucky or unlucky? Ask them to explain their thinking.

- Joey tells us that he was happy despite being 'in the middle of a nightmare'. What is the nightmare he is speaking about, and what makes him feel happy?

- Emilie is the first female to have helped care for Joey. In what ways is she 'a special child' for him and Topthorn?

- Invite the children to suggest what next might be in store for Joey. At the end of Chapter 10, Emilie's grandfather says that 'All's well'. Does this mean Joey and Topthorn will remain with them at the farm and the war will end?

Ask the children, whenever appropriate, to revisit the text to exemplify/support their answers.

Encourage the children to read aloud back to the group when referring back to the text – praise clear, confident and expressive reading.

## Before the next session

Ask the children to read Chapters 11 and 12, comparing their predictions with what actually happens next in the story.

## ASSESSMENT OPPORTUNITIES

The following bank of question prompts provides a quick and easy means of monitoring the children's comprehension skills and understanding of the text. The children's answers to a question must be supported by evidence from the text.

### Understanding

- What job were Joey and Topthorn doing while they were at the German field hospital?
- Why did the German soldier hang his Iron Cross medal round Joey's neck?
- While they were at the hospital, who looked after Joey and Topthorn each evening when their work was finished?
- What was the little girl's name?
- What did Emilie and her grandfather do each evening, to care for Joey and Topthorn?
- What two things did Joey think made it possible for himself and Topthorn to get through each day?
- What did Emilie do every night before she went to sleep? How do we know?
- When she became ill, what was wrong with Emilie?
- What effect did the snow have on Joey and Topthorn pulling the cart?
- What did the soldiers do when they realised it was Christmas morning?
- What did Joey and Topthorn get for Christmas?

### Inferences

- Why would marching soldiers cheer as Joey and Topthorn passed, hauling dying and wounded men?
- How do we know that Emilie and her grandfather were used to horses?
- How do we know that Emilie expected to keep the horses after the war?
- Why did Joey say that any horse 'has a fondness for children'?

- How do we know the horses were special for Emilie? Why might this have been?
- How did Joey and Topthorn know that something was wrong after they got back on the first snowy day of winter?
- Why did Emilie live alone with her grandfather?
- What special present did Emilie's grandfather get?
- Why do you think the last night in the chapter was quiet?

### Predicting

- Emilie says she will keep the horses when the war is over. Do you think she will? Explain why.

### Main ideas

- In what ways does the author show us that the experiences of war are the same for both sides?

### Language, structure and presentation

- What is 'the front line'?
- What is 'No-Man's Land'?

### Themes and conventions

- We see Joey in the care of several owners during the course of the story. In what ways are they similar?

# SESSION 5: THE WAR MARCHES ON

## SESSION AIMS

Consider the ways in which the war affects different characters.

Identify similarities in some of Joey's experiences.

## READ

- When the German soldiers moved the field hospital, why did they allow Joey and Topthorn to remain on the farm with Emilie and her grandfather? What jobs did the horses do now, and how do we know that Joey enjoyed this change in his life?

- Invite the children to identify ways in which Joey's life with Emilie and her grandfather was similar to his life before the war with Albert.

- Can the children explain why Emilie would find losing the horses particularly difficult? (She has already lost her brother and parents to the war.)

- Ask the children to describe the differences in Joey and Topthorn's life when they are with the artillery after they leave the farm.

- We can see how important horses were to the army, and yet they don't always get the best treatment. Can the children suggest why this might be?

- Do the children think that knowing the fate of many other horses would have an effect on Joey and Topthorn? Ask them to explain.

- Can the children suggest why Michael Morpurgo writes such vivid and upsetting descriptions of life for the horses?

- Invite the children to suggest what might happen to Topthorn.

- Were they correct in any of their predictions for Chapters 11 and 12.

### During reading

- Ask the children to read Chapter 13 in the next part of the session. Ask them to concentrate on the character of Friedrich, considering his opinions about the war.

- If your school uses reading journals then the children should be encouraged to make notes as they read and consider each question.

- Move around the group and 'tune in' to hear individuals read aloud. Encourage and praise good expression.

## REVISIT AND RESPOND

Use the following discussion points to help the children think about what they have read in more depth.

**Note:** Since there are only 20 minutes for each session, you are advised to focus on only one or two of the elements that are listed below.

- Invite the children to suggest reasons why the men treated the horses better when spring came. In what ways did the horses benefit?

- Ask the children to discuss the character of Friedrich. Ask them to find examples in the text to show us what he is like, and why Joey and Topthorn trusted him.

- The soldiers call him 'mad old Friedrich' but he thinks he is 'the only sane man in the regiment'. Do the children agree? What message is the author giving by including Friedrich? (He is showing us that even some of the people involved feel the war is not worth fighting; that it is not how people should behave towards each other.)

- We have read about Topthorn becoming weak and ill because Joey tells us about what happens. Invite the children to suggest how his illness might affect Topthorn's feelings – what might he think? If Topthorn was telling the story, what might he say about this period?

Ask the children, whenever appropriate, to revisit the text to exemplify/support their answers.

Encourage the children to read aloud back to the group when referring back to the text – praise clear, confident and expressive reading.

### Before the next session

To prepare for the next session, ask the children to read Chapters 14 and 15, considering how the events make them feel.

## ASSESSMENT OPPORTUNITIES

The following bank of question prompts provides a quick and easy means of monitoring the children's comprehension skills and understanding of the text. The children's answers to a question must be supported by evidence from the text.

### Understanding

- In what ways did Topthorn still suffer after his illness during the winter?
- In what ways did Joey and Topthorn's health improve in the spring? Why?
- How did Joey and Topthorn spend that summer? What job did they do now?
- Who now took care of Joey and Topthorn?
- Why was Friedrich known as 'mad old Friedrich'?
- Why was Friedrich given the jobs to do that no one else wanted to do?
- Why did Joey and Topthorn lose the weight they had gained?
- What did Friedrich do to make Joey and Topthorn's trips from the railhead easier?
- What job had Friedrich done before the war?
- What reason did Friedrich give for talking to himself?
- What reason does Friedrich give for not marching away from the war, as he would like to do?

### Inferences

- What reasons did Joey and Topthorn have for realising Friedrich was not mad at all?
- Why did Joey think Friedrich preferred Topthorn?
- How do we know the German soldiers thought the war might end soon?
- Friedrich told the horses that if he didn't laugh he would cry. Why would this be?

- We know that Friedrich doesn't really want to be part of the war. How does he manage to cope with being a part of it?
- Why do you think Friedrich would often 'stand back and gaze at Topthorn... with love and glowing admiration in his eyes'?

### Predicting

- What do you think is going to happen to Topthorn?

### Main ideas

- Explain why Friedrich thought he was 'the only sane one in the regiment'.
- Joey is moved between people, places and jobs. Explain how he manages to cope with all these changes. What helps him in each new placement?
- Give some reasons why Joey and Topthorn have grown to become such close companions.

### Language, structure and presentation

- What are 'Haflingers'?
- Joey is in the care of yet another person. How does his moving between carers help the story to build?
- Friedrich calls the war 'benighted'. What does this mean?

# SESSION 6: NO MAN'S LAND

## SESSION AIMS

Consider the effects of the writing upon the reader. Identify key themes of the story.

## BEFORE THE SESSION

The children should have read Chapters 14 and 15 prior to the session.

## READ

- The events described in Chapters 14 and 15 may have been upsetting for some children, particularly reading of the deaths of Topthorn and Friedrich. Invite the children to talk about how reading these two chapters made them feel. Can they explain why they felt this way? What does this tell us about the quality of the writing and the skill of the author?

- Ask the children to identify examples in the opening of Chapter 14 where a calm atmosphere is described. Compare this with the end of the chapter when the shelling begins.

- Can they find examples of assonance in the opening of Chapter 14 ('silver glinting river'; 'sat, back, flat') and alliteration ('welcome...water')?

- What did the children notice about the way Rudi spoke about horses? He is very articulate and knowledgeable. Is this how we normally think of the voice of a soldier?

- Can the children explain why Joey felt he had to stay beside the bodies of Topthorn and Friedrich? What might have happened if the tanks hadn't arrived to make him bolt away?

- What do the children think Albert and Emilie's reactions would be if they knew what was happening to Joey?

### During reading

- Ask the children to read Chapter 16. This is another very moving chapter where there is finally some relief for Joey from his recent traumas. As they read,

ask the children to think about the responses of the soldiers who come to Joey's aid.

- If your school uses reading journals then the children should be encouraged to make notes as they read and consider each question.

- Move around the group and 'tune in' to hear individuals read aloud. Encourage and praise good expression.

## REVISIT AND RESPOND

Use the following discussion points to help the children think about what they have read in more depth.

**Note:** Since there are only 20 minutes for each session, you are advised to focus on only one or two of the elements that are listed below.

- Ask the children how they felt when they realised that Joey's recent ordeal seemed to be over, giving their reasons.

- Why do they think that soldiers from both sides were keen to rescue Joey? Was it: because they really needed another horse; because they could see he was an animal who had suffered and they wanted to help him; because it was a relief from the incessant battle, or a mixture of all three?

- How might Joey feel when he sees the two soldiers approaching him? Why?

- Ask the children: *What is shown by the fact that both sets of soldiers want to rescue Joey and the conversation between the two soldiers who go across No-Man's Land?* Explore with them how this suggests the war was the same for both sides; also, both men saw it as futile to be fighting and killing each other. Here the author seems to give the message that it is not the troops who want to fight but those in charge far above them. The two men co-operate to rescue Joey. Invite the children to discuss their thoughts about the soldiers' perspective.

Ask the children, whenever appropriate, to revisit the text to exemplify/support their answers.

Encourage the children to read aloud back to the group when referring back to the text – praise clear, confident and expressive reading.

### Before the next session
Ask the children to read Chapters 17 and 18. As they read, ask the children to identify how tension is built as the events unfold.

## ASSESSMENT OPPORTUNITIES
The following bank of question prompts provides a quick and easy means of monitoring the children's comprehension skills and understanding of the text. The children's answers to a question must be supported by evidence from the text.

### Understanding
- What did Joey hear that made him realise it was real people nearby?
- What did Joey smell when he was in No-Man's Land?
- Who was on either side of Joey when he was in No-Man's Land?
- Why did Joey want to move towards the smell of food? What stopped him?
- How long did Joey spend trying to get out of No-Man's Land?
- How was the soldier with the white flag able to get to Joey?
- What happened next after the soldier with the white flag came out of the trench?
- Who did the German soldier remind Joey of?
- What were the differences between the two soldiers who came to rescue Joey?
- What did the German soldier bring for Joey?
- How were the British and German soldiers able to communicate?
- Why did the German soldier think he should have Joey?
- How did the soldiers decide who should take Joey?
- Why did the German soldier hold up the coin to show both sides?

### Inferences
- How do we know in the opening of the chapter that there is no fighting?
- Why do you think the soldiers cheered Joey as he tried to reach them?
- What does it mean when a soldier waves a white flag?
- Would it make any difference to Joey which side rescued him? Give reasons for your answer.
- What does the reference to King Solomon's solution have for the two soldiers? If you don't know, try to find out.
- How do we know a German coin was used for the toss?
- How do you think Joey would feel being won by the British?

### Predicting
- What do you think will happen now that Joey is back in the care of the British troops?

### Main ideas
- What did the German soldier say that he and the British soldier had shown people by their actions? Why is this an important speech for the story as a whole?

### Language, structure and presentation
- Why is the section between the enemy lines known as 'No-Man's Land'?
- Why did the British soldier call the German 'Jerry'?

### Themes and conventions
- A continuing theme of the story is how terrible war is for both sides and for all involved. Explain what you think the author's views are about war, based on this.

# SESSION 7: REUNITED

## SESSION AIMS

Identify how the author builds tension.

## BEFORE THE SESSION

The children should have read Chapters 17 and 18 prior to the session.

## READ

- Ask the children: *How do we know that the story of Joey's rescue spread?* (For example: soldiers came to greet him at the hospital; Sergeant Thunder mentioned it.)

- Ask the children for their first reactions to Sergeant Thunder, giving their reasons. Why was he called 'Thunder'? Is there any good reason for him to speak as he does? (There were over 100 horses and only 12 men to care for them, and he had to lead and organise them.) Did the children's opinion of Sergeant Thunder change at all later and if so, why?

- Can the children explain how it helped the tension of the story that Joey was covered in mud and blood?

- How would it have affected the story if Albert had recognised Joey straightaway?

- Ask the children to give examples of how the author has built the tension, for example the slow reveal to Albert that the horse he was helping to clean was Joey; the clear description Albert gave to David; the fact that Albert was cleaning the rear of the horse so that David was the one to see Joey gradually emerge, Albert not believing David at first when he said he thought the horse was Joey.

- How do the children think Joey would feel, trying to show Albert who he was?

- What was the final thing that made Albert certain that the horse was Joey?

- How did David persuade Major Martin to try and save Joey when he had tetanus?

- Joey tells us what happened to him and about

his symptoms, but not how he felt or what he thought. Why do the children think the author didn't include this?

### During reading

- Ask the children to read Chapter 19. As they read, ask them to note Joey's various experiences and how they affect him.

- If your school uses reading journals then the children should be encouraged to make notes as they read and consider each question.

- Move around the group and 'tune in' to hear individuals read aloud. Encourage and praise good expression.

## REVISIT AND RESPOND

Use the following discussion points to help the children think about what they have read in more depth.

**Note:** Since there are only 20 minutes for each session, you are advised to focus on only one or two of the elements that are listed below.

- In what ways do we see Joey and Albert re-establishing their friendship?

- What was the one thing about Joey that Albert found frustrating (the fact that Joey couldn't talk to Albert)? The fact we, as readers, 'hear' Joey's voice puts us in a unique position. Ask the children: *If you were able to tell Albert what you knew from Joey himself, what would you tell Albert?*

- The end of the war is underplayed and anti-climactic. Invite the children to explain why they think this might have been.

- How did the children feel when they read that the horses were not going to be taken back home when the soldiers left? Do they understand Major Martin's reasons for this decision?

- Invite the children to predict what will happen next. Will some way be found for Joey to go home? Will Albert find a way to stay with him in France?

Ask the children, whenever appropriate, to revisit the text to exemplify/support their answers.

Encourage the children to read aloud back to the group when referring back to the text – praise clear, confident and expressive reading.

### Before the next session

In preparation for the final session, ask the children to read Chapter 20. Encourage them to consider Albert's feelings during the events described.

## ASSESSMENT OPPORTUNITIES

The following bank of question prompts provides a quick and easy means of monitoring the children's comprehension skills and understanding of the text. The children's answers to a question must be supported by evidence from the text.

### Understanding

- What job did Joey do when he first started to get better?
- Who had arranged for Albert to work with Joey?
- What job did Albert do when he wasn't working with Joey?
- How did Albert's occasional absence affect Joey?
- What role did Joey play when he was fully recovered?
- What stopped Joey from feeling afraid of the guns?
- How did Albert make Joey feel protected when they went to the front line?
- What did Albert tell Joey his girlfriend was good at?
- What did Albert's girlfriend think about him joining the army to go to France?
- What had Albert's friend David done before the war?
- What did Albert tell Joey he would do when they got home?
- What did Joey do to try and comfort Albert?
- What did Major Martin say was going to happen to the horses?
- What reason did Major Martin give for the horses staying in France?

### Inferences

- What terrible news did Albert receive? How did it affect him?
- How did news of the end of the war affect the men?

- Why do you think there was an increase in sick and wounded horses at the veterinary hospital after the war ended?
- Sergeant Thunder and Major Martin knew what would probably happen to the horses after they had been sold. What do you think they knew would happen?
- How did Major Martin and Sergeant Thunder feel about having to sell the horses? How do you know?
- How do you think Albert would feel about Joey being sold?
- What would Joey feel about being sold and staying in France?
- What does the number of horses involved tell you about how much they were needed during the war?

### Predicting

- What do you think will happen at the horse auction?

### Main ideas

- We have seen throughout the story the importance of horses in the war. What are your opinions about the army deciding to sell them and leave them in France? Give your reasons.

### Language, structure and presentation

- How does Sergeant Thunder appear now, compared to the first time we met him? In what ways does his language and manner of speech show us how he has changed?

# SESSION 8: GOING HOME

Suggest reasons for characters' actions.
Identify the main ideas underpinning the story.

## BEFORE THE SESSION

The children should have read Chapter 20 prior to the session.

## READ

- The opening paragraph talks of an atmosphere of 'determined conspiracy'. Ask the children to identify ways in which Michael Morpurgo explains what this means later in the paragraph.

- Why do they think Albert took no notice of Joey on the day of the preparations for the auction, apart from jerking sharply at his halter? What do his actions show us about Albert's feelings?

- Ask the children what the plan was that Sergeant Thunder was organising. Ask them: *What does it show you about him and about what all the men felt about Joey? Why do you think Joey had become so special to everyone?*

- Albert told Joey that he couldn't tell him anything about what was being planned. Why was this? Why did he feel he couldn't promise Joey anything, especially when he had made an unlikely promise to him many years before? Do the children remember what that promise was? (When he said he would come to France and find Joey.)

- Why would the sale to the butcher have been so devastating for everyone?

- Who was the only one there who knew who Emilie and the mysterious French buyer were?

- How would the sale to the final bidder affect Sergeant Thunder, Albert and the other soldiers? (For example, they knew nothing about Joey's life with Emilie and her grandfather so wouldn't understand why the old man was so eager to buy Joey.)

- Invite the children to predict what will happen in the final chapter, now that Emilie's grandfather has bought Joey.

### During reading

- Ask the children to read the final chapter. As they read, ask them to think how Joey would feel as events unfold.

- If your school uses reading journals then the children should be encouraged to make notes as they read and consider each question.

- Move around the group and 'tune in' to hear individuals read aloud. Encourage and praise good expression.

## REVISIT AND RESPOND

Use the following discussion points to help the children think about what they have read in more depth.

**Note:** Since there are only 20 minutes for each session, you are advised to focus on only one or two of the elements that are listed below.

- Several major things happen to Joey at and after the auction, in quick succession. Ask the children to recall what these events are (Joey is auctioned; seems to be being sold to a butcher; is finally bought by Emilie's grandfather who he knows; then is given back to Albert). Suggest how this rollercoaster of events would make him feel.

- How do they think these same events would affect Albert?

- Why do the children think that Major Martin and Sergeant Thunder said they didn't know what Albert was talking about when he thanked them for what they did to save Joey? Why did they not accept Albert's thanks?

- Ask the children why they think it was important for Emilie's grandfather to tell Albert the whole story about the time Joey and Topthorn spent with them.

- Ask the children to suggest what messages about war the author has made in telling the story.

Ask the children, whenever appropriate, to revisit the text to exemplify/support their answers.

Encourage the children to read aloud back to the group when referring back to the text – praise clear, confident and expressive reading.

## ASSESSMENT OPPORTUNITIES

The following bank of question prompts provides a quick and easy means of monitoring the children's comprehension skills and understanding of the text. The children's answers to a question must be supported by evidence from the text.

### Understanding

- What did Albert's friends say to try to make him feel better about Joey being sold to the old man?
- How did Albert's friends know that Emilie's grandfather would give Joey a good life?
- Why did Albert want to speak to 'the Frenchman'?
- In what ways were Albert and Emilie's grandfather similar?
- What did Albert tell Emilie's grandfather was kept on his farm?
- What effect did Joey and Topthorn's leaving have on Emilie?
- What did Emilie ask her grandfather to promise?
- What reason did Grandfather give to Albert for farmers never giving anything away?
- What reasons did Grandfather give for offering Joey to Albert?
- How much did Grandfather charge Albert for Joey? Why do you think he did that?
- What promise did Albert have to give Grandfather in accepting Joey?
- Why was Albert's promise important to Grandfather?
- What did Grandfather mockingly accuse Albert of?
- Who produced the penny to pay for Joey?
- What did Grandfather say he would do with the penny?
- How were Albert and Joey greeted on their arrival back home?
- Who did Joey say were the real heroes? Why did he say this?

- What happened to Albert after they came home?
- What reason did Joey give for Maisie Cobbledick not liking him much?
- What job did Joey do when he got back home?

### Inferences

- How do you think Emilie's grandfather seemed to know that Joey would be at the auction?
- How do we know that Major Martin had been told Emilie's grandfather's story?
- Why do you think Major Martin would tell Emilie's grandfather Albert's story?
- How do we know that Grandfather didn't know that Topthorn had been killed?
- Why did Albert not speak in answer to Grandfather's offer?
- Why did it not matter that Albert didn't answer Grandfather when he offered him Joey?
- How did Albert and Grandfather each know that Albert would carry out the promise?
- Why do you think Grandfather didn't want the £28 he had paid for Joey?
- How would Albert and Joey feel at the greeting they received when they got home?
- How had Albert's father changed since the start of the story?

### Main ideas

- Do you think the book was successful in showing how horses were used in the First World War? Explain your answer.

### Language, structure and presentation

- What did Emilie's grandfather mean when he called Albert 'Tommy'?
- Why do you think it was important for the story to cover the whole period of the war?

### Themes and conventions

- The story is told through the voice of Joey. What differences would there be if the story had been told in the third person?
- What do you think is Michael Morpurgo's view of war, as it is described in the book?

# ▼ GUIDED READING RECORD

| Year | | Term | |
|------|------|------|------|
| Group | | Reading target | |

| Date | Text | Objectives | Names | Comments |
|------|------|------------|-------|----------|
| | | | | |
| | | | | |
| | | | | |
| | | | | |
| | | | | |
| | | | | |
| | | | | |
| | | | | |

| Notes |
|-------|
| |

**SCHOLASTIC**

# READ & RESPOND

Bringing the best books to life in the classroom

**SCHOLASTIC**

# READ & RESPOND

Bringing the best books to life in the classroom

## BOOK:

...........................................

...........................................

...........................................

...........................................

...........................................

...........................................

...........................................

...........................................

...........................................

...........................................

...........................................

...........................................

## BOOK:

...........................................

...........................................

...........................................

...........................................

...........................................

...........................................

...........................................

...........................................

...........................................

...........................................

...........................................

...........................................

# SCHOLASTIC

# READ & RESPOND

## Bringing the best books to life in the classroom

### Plan with confidence

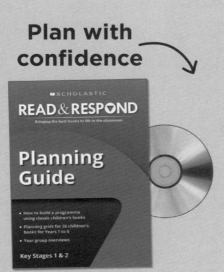

The Planning Guide provides a teaching structure for Years 1–6.

### Boost guided reading time

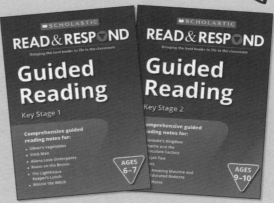

Six guided reading books are available, for Years 1–6.

### Teach the best children's books

A huge range of Teacher's Books are available for Years 1–6.

### Engage every reader

Children's books are available in sets of 6 and 30.

Order at www.scholastic.co.uk/readandrespond
or call us on 0845 6039091